EASY PIANO

INSPIRATIONAL BALLADS

INDEXED IN SONG INDEX

20 SONGS OF FAITH, HOPE & LOVE

ISBN 978-1-4234-3831-1

HAL•LEONARD®
CORPORATION

7777 W. BLUEMOUND RD. P.O. BOX 13819 MILWAUKEE, WI 53213

Visit Hal Leonard Online at
www.halleonard.com

CONTENTS

ALWAYS THERE

Words and Music by BRENDAN GRAHAM
and ROLF LOVLAND

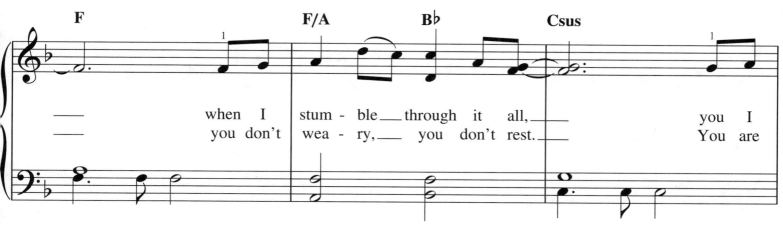

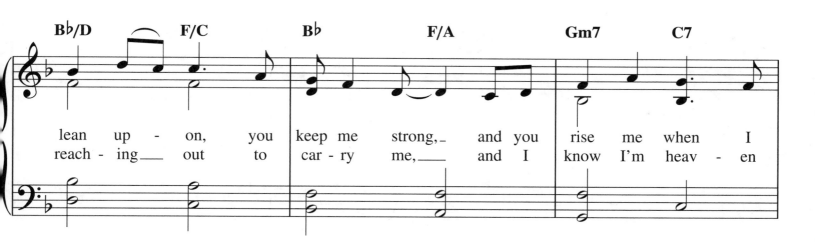

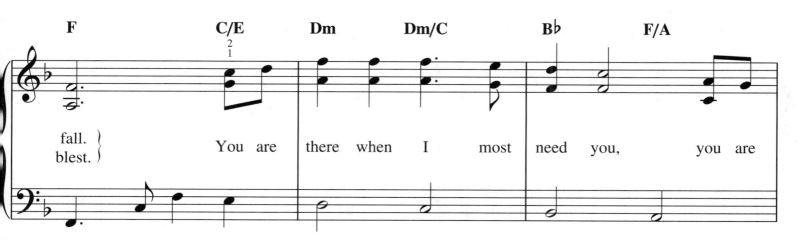

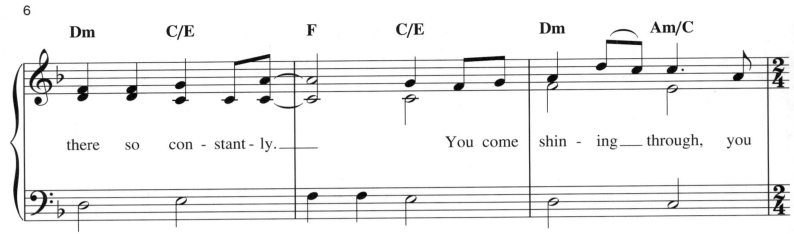

there so con - stant - ly. ___ You come shin - ing __ through, you

al - ways do, you are al - ways there for

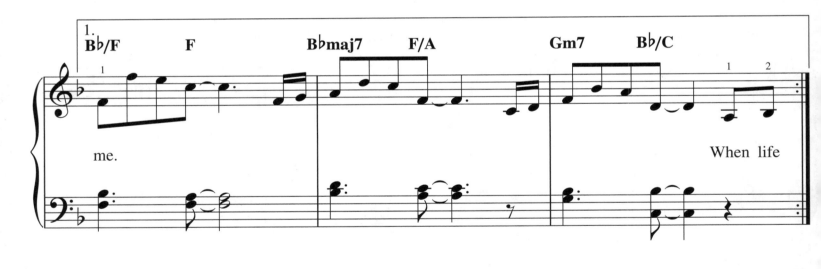

1.

me. When life

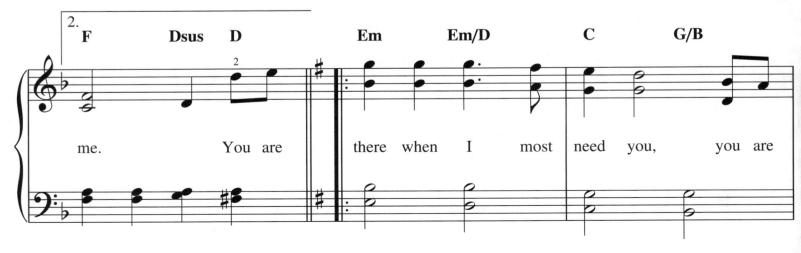

2.

me. You are there when I most need you, you are

FRIENDS

Words and Music by MICHAEL W. SMITH
and DEBORAH D. SMITH

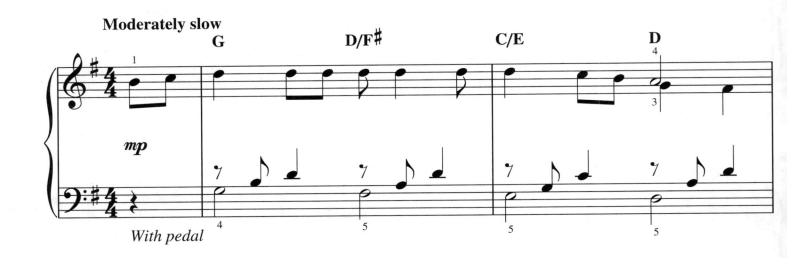

Pack-ing up__ the dreams   God
With the faith__ and love   God's

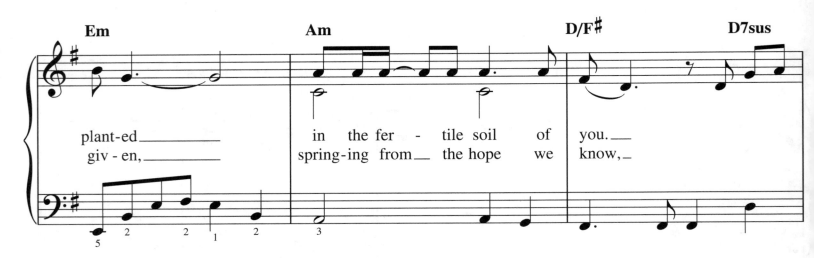

plant-ed_____   in the fer - tile soil   of   you.__
giv - en,_____   spring-ing from__ the hope   we   know,__

11

BLESS THE BROKEN ROAD

Words and Music by MARCUS HUMMON,
BOBBY BOYD and JEFF HANNA

14

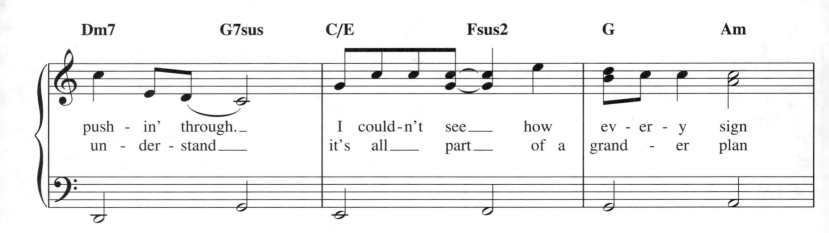

point - ed straight___ to you.
that is com - in' true. But ev - er - y
Ev - er - y

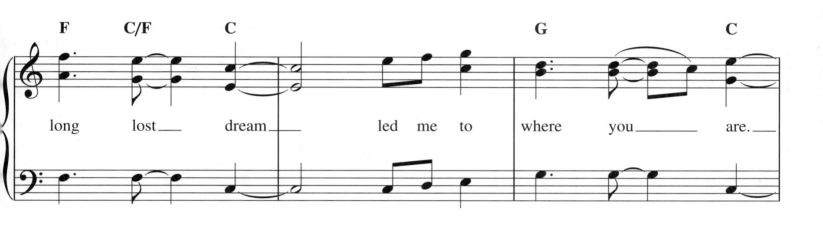

long lost___ dream___ led me to where you_____ are.___

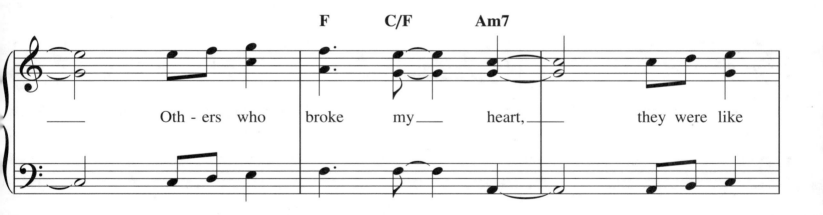

___ Oth - ers who broke my___ heart,___ they were like

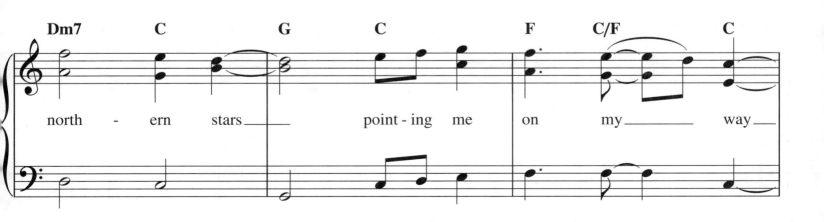

north - ern stars___ point - ing me on my_____ way___

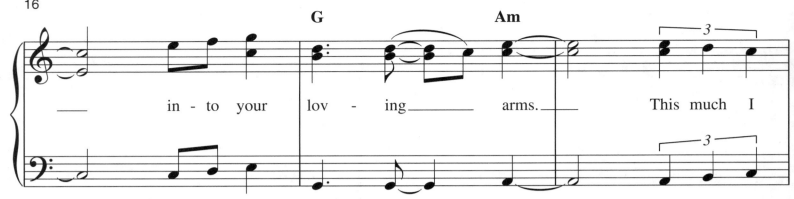

into your loving arms. This much I

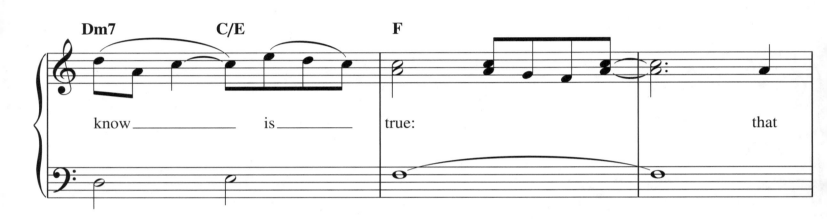

know is true: that

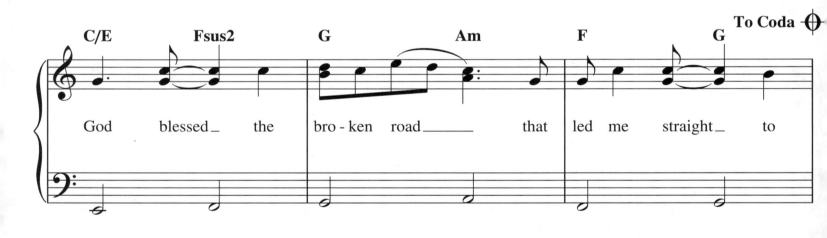

God blessed the broken road that led me straight to

you.

true: that God blessed_ the

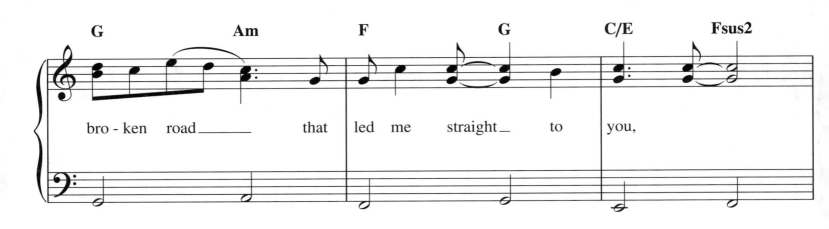

bro - ken road_____ that led me straight_ to you,

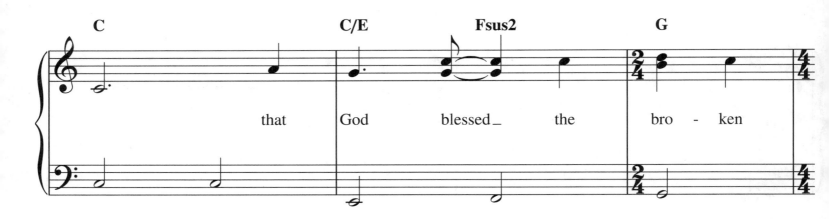

that God blessed_ the bro - ken

FROM A DISTANCE

Words and Music by
JULIE GOLD

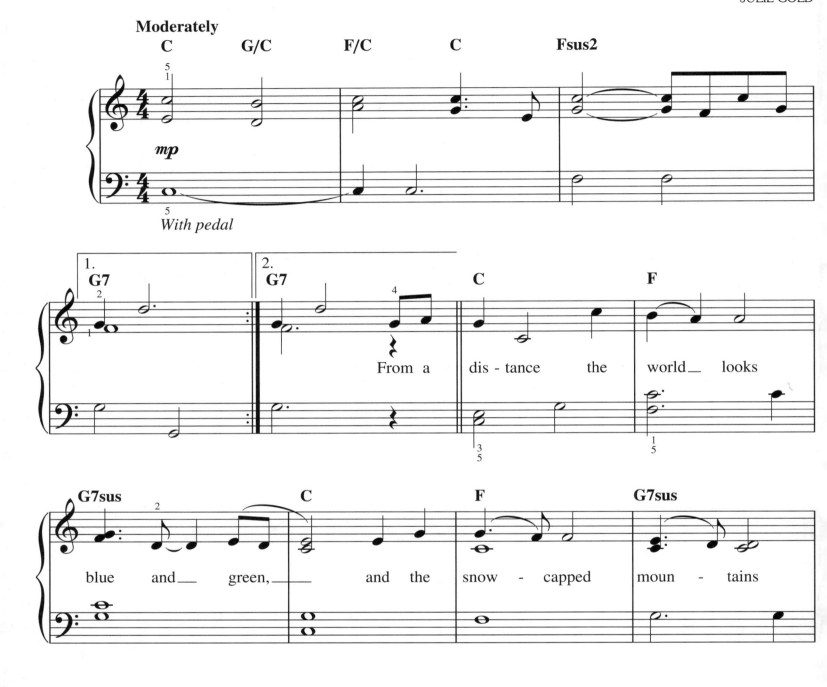

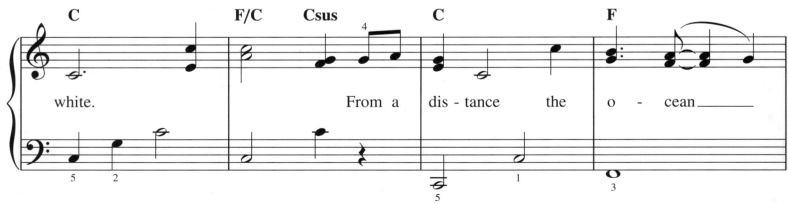

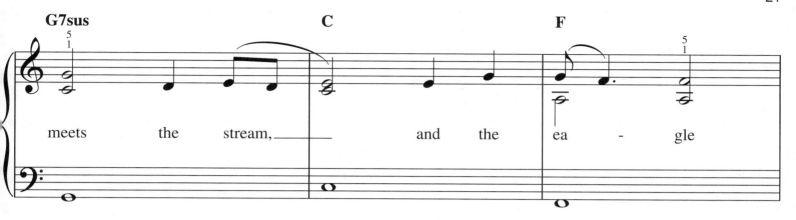

meets   the   stream, _____   and   the   ea - gle

takes _____   to   flight.   From ___ a

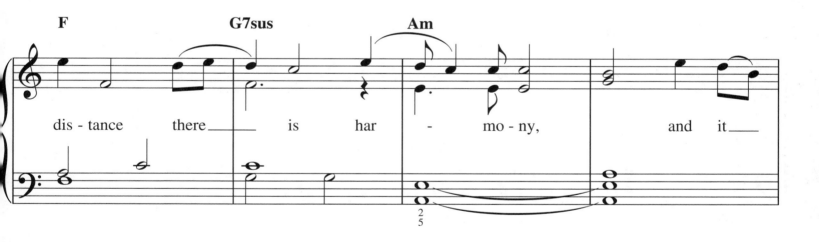

dis - tance   there ___   is   har - mo - ny,   and   it ___

ech - oes   through   the   land. _____   It's   the

22

voice of____ hope,_____ it's the voice of____

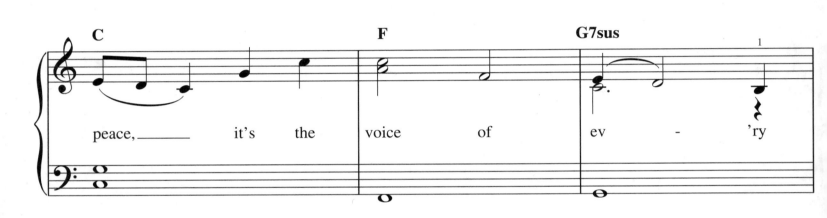

peace,_____ it's the voice of ev - 'ry

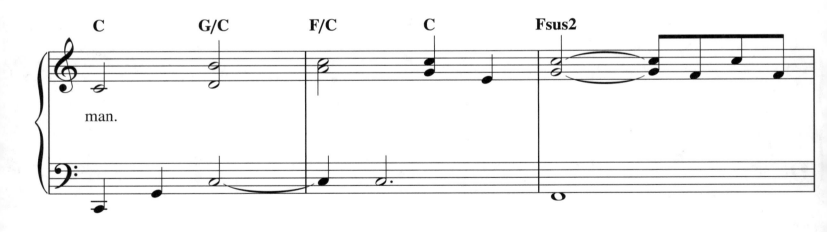

man.

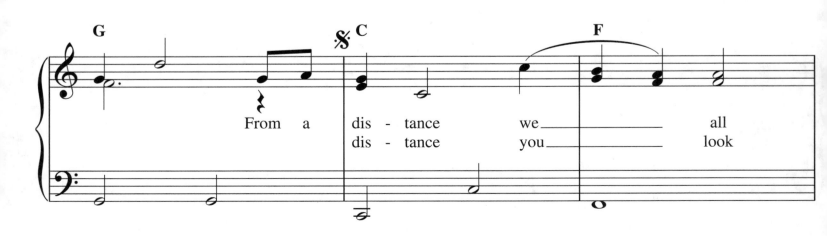

From a dis - tance we_____ all
dis - tance you_____ look

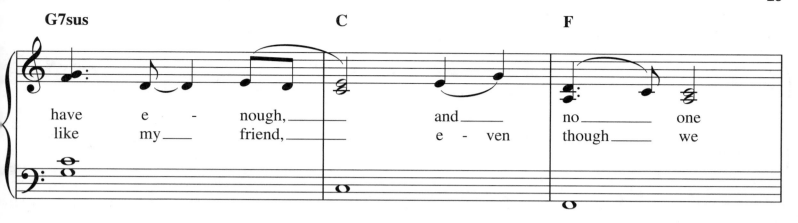

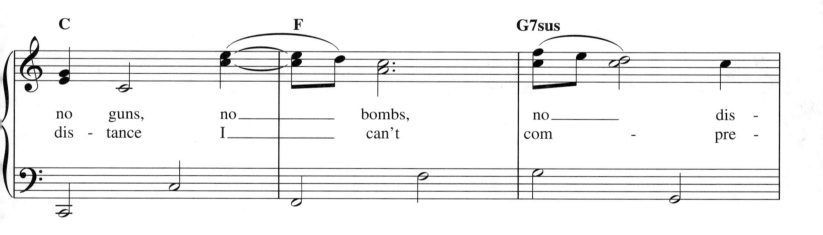

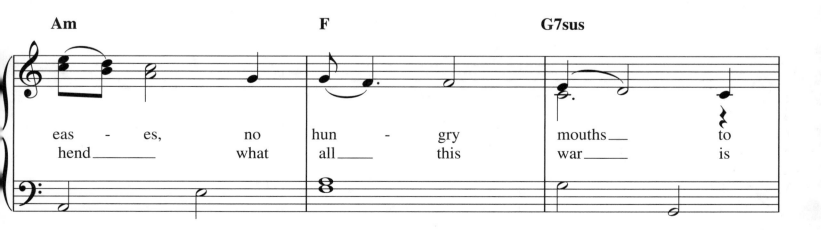

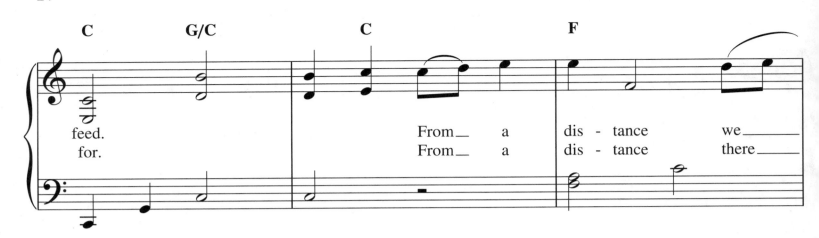

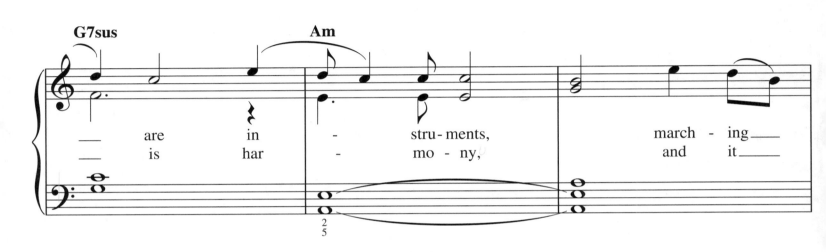

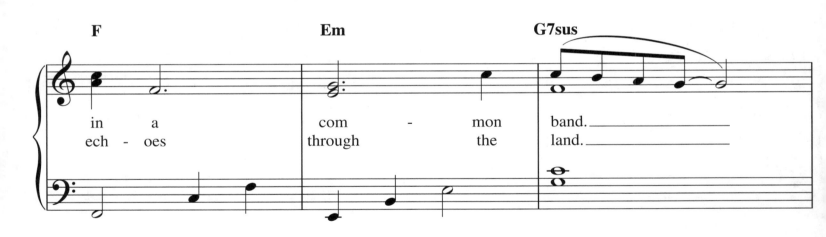

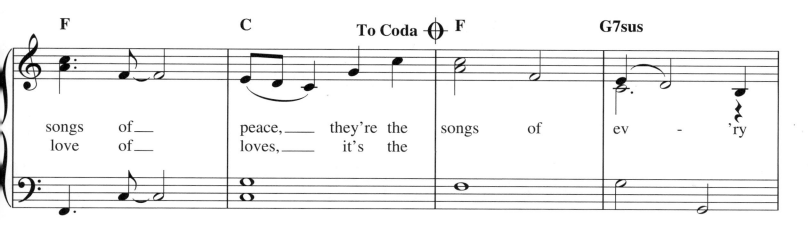

songs of ___ peace, ___ they're the songs of ev - 'ry
love of ___ loves, ___ it's the

man. God ___ is watch - ing us, ___ God ___ is

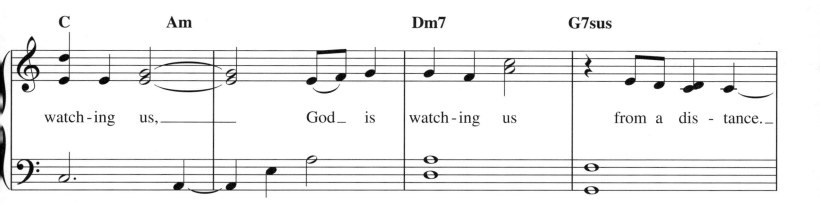

watch - ing us, ___ God ___ is watch - ing us from a dis - tance. ___

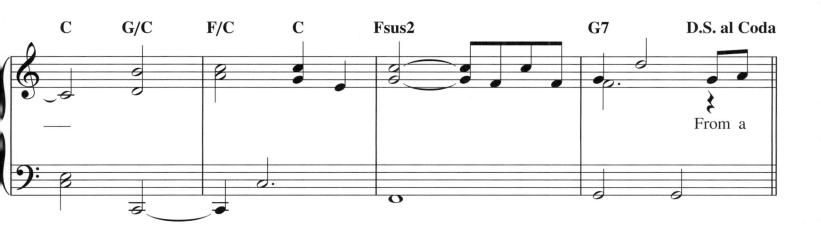

From a

CODA

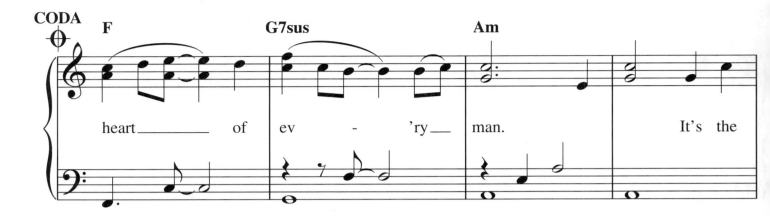

heart _____ of ev - 'ry ___ man. It's the

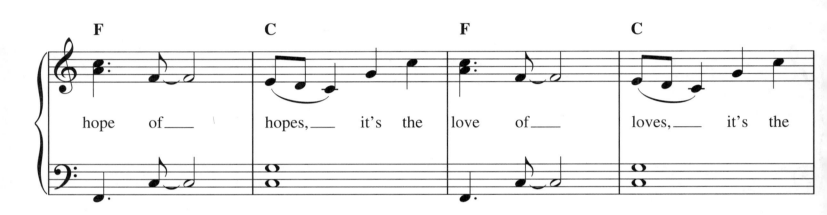

hope of ___ hopes, ___ it's the love of ___ loves, ___ it's the

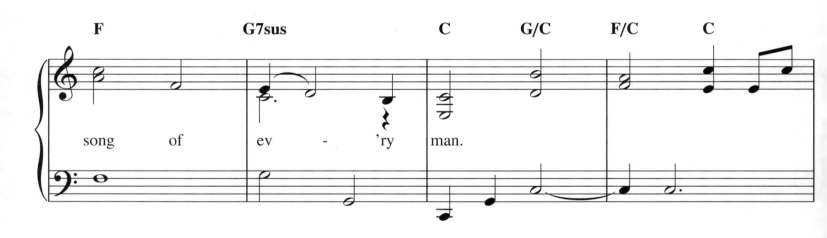

song of ev - 'ry man.

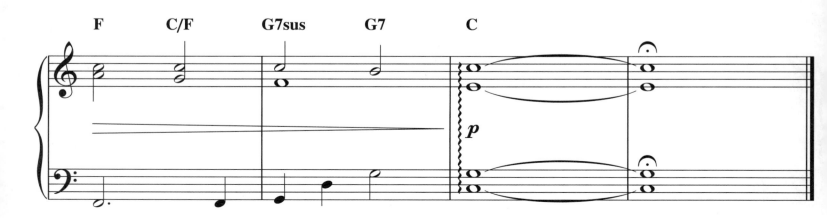

I CAN ONLY IMAGINE

Words and Music by
BART MILLARD

I can on-ly i-

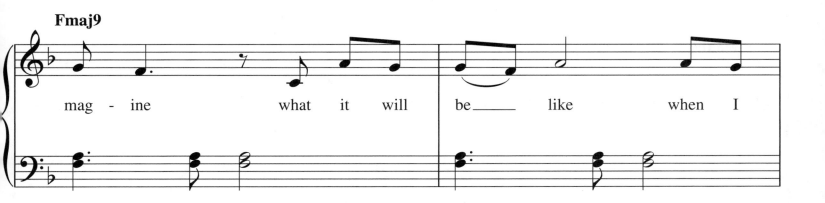

mag- ine what it will be___ like when I

B♭maj9

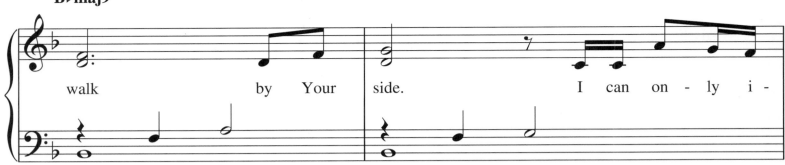

walk   by Your   side.   I can on - ly i -

Fmaj9

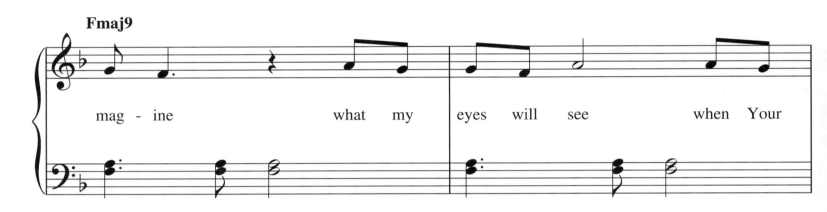

mag - ine   what my   eyes will see   when Your

B♭maj9

face   is be - fore me.   I can on - ly i -

Fmaj9

mag - ine.____

B♭maj9

Sur -

B♭sus2 ... **C**

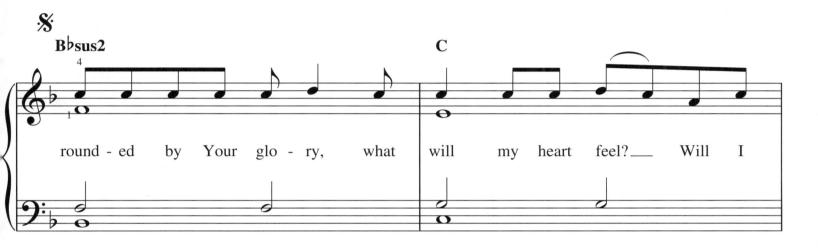

round - ed by Your glo - ry, what will my heart feel?___ Will I

F

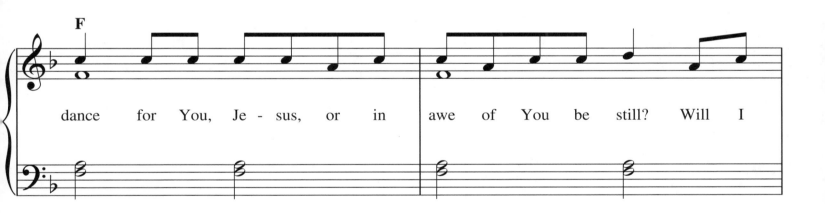

dance for You, Je - sus, or in awe of You be still? Will I

B♭sus2 ... **C**

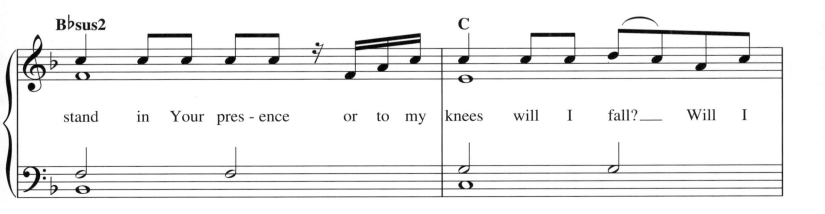

stand in Your pres - ence or to my knees will I fall?___ Will I

F

sing hal - le - lu - jah? Will I be a - ble to speak at all? I can on - ly i-

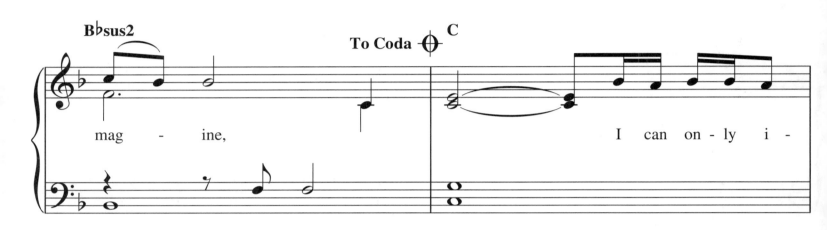

B♭sus2   **To Coda** ⊕ **C**

mag - ine,   I can on - ly i-

Fmaj7

mag - ine.___   I can on - ly i-

Fmaj9

mag - ine   when that   day   comes   and I

B♭maj9 — find my - self stand - ing **C7sus** — in the Son. I can on - ly i-

Fmaj9 — mag - ine when all I will do is for -

B♭maj9 — ev - er, for - ev - er **C7sus** — wor - ship You. I can on - ly i-

Fmaj9 — mag - ine.___ I can on - ly i-

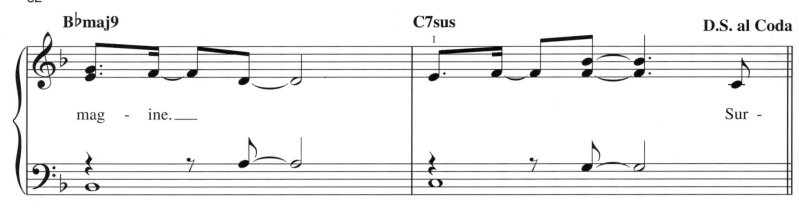

mag - ine.___ Sur -

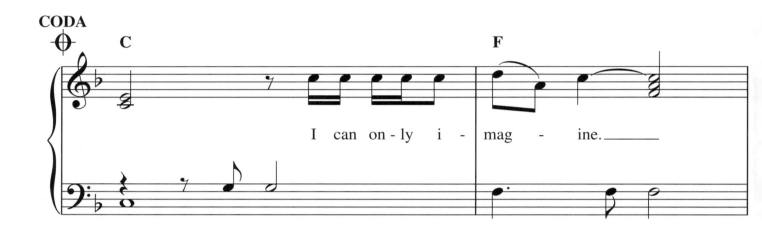

I can on - ly i - mag - ine.___

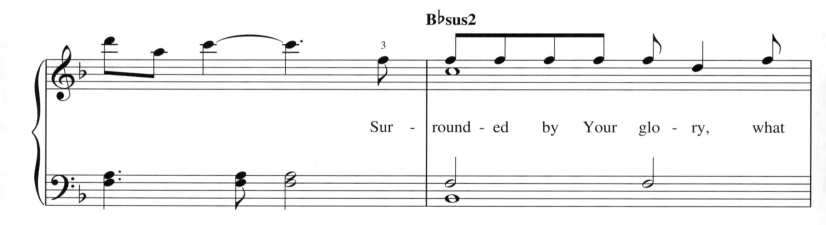

Sur - round - ed by Your glo - ry, what

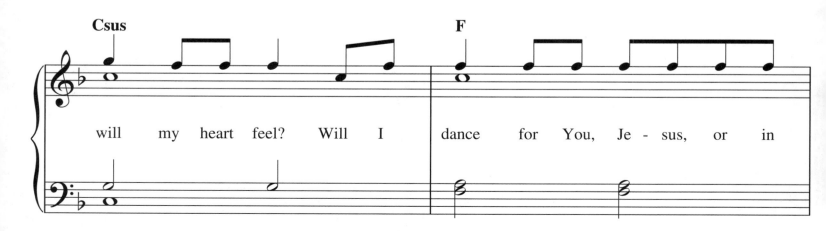

will my heart feel? Will I dance for You, Je - sus, or in

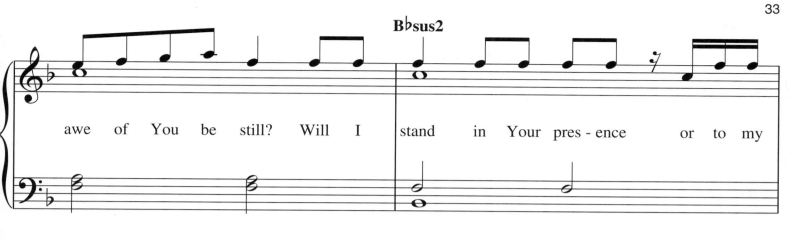

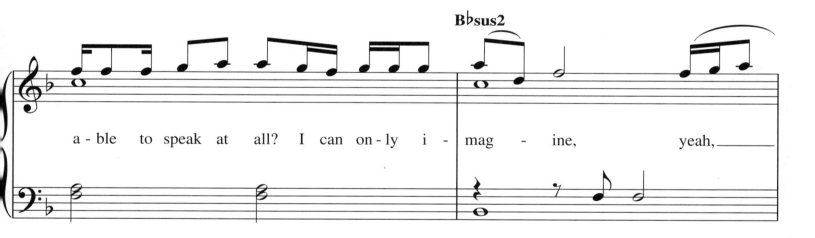

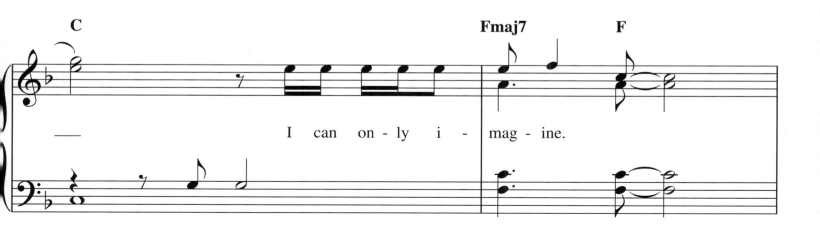

I can on-ly i - mag-ine, yeah, _____

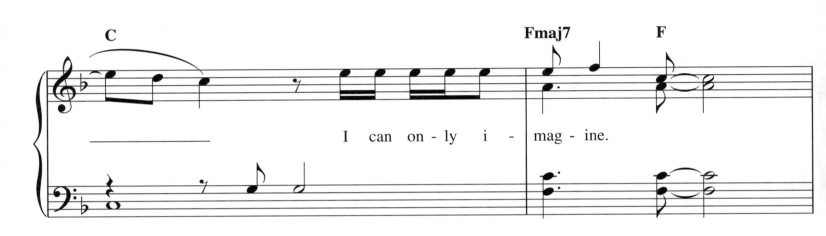

_____ I can on-ly i - mag - ine.

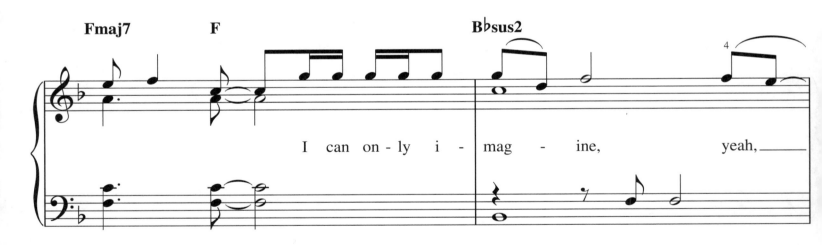

I can on-ly i - mag - ine, yeah, _____

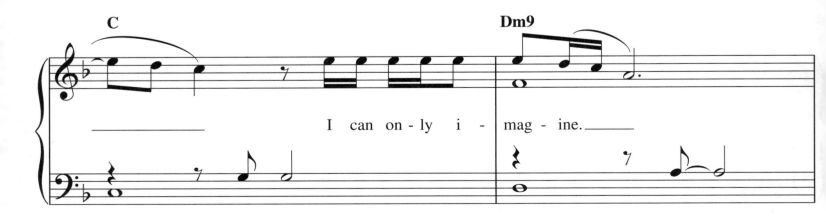

_____ I can on-ly i - mag - ine. _____

I can on - ly i - mag - ine_____ when all

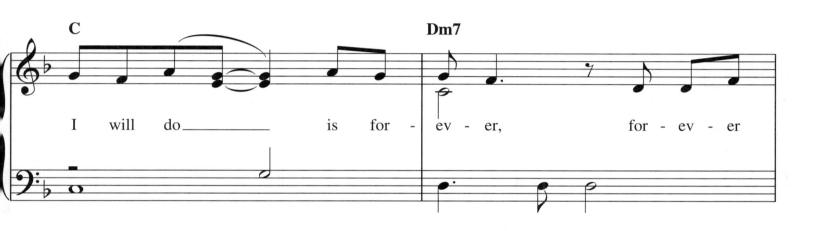

I will do_____ is for - ev - er, for - ev - er

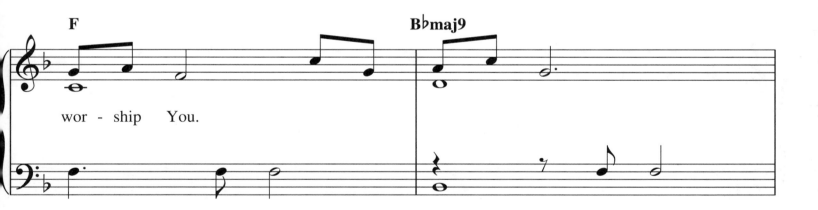

wor - ship You.

I can on - ly i - mag - ine._____

GOD BLESS THE U.S.A.

Words and Music by
LEE GREENWOOD

And I'm proud to be an A-mer-i-can___ where at

least I know I'm free. And I won't for-get the men who died, who

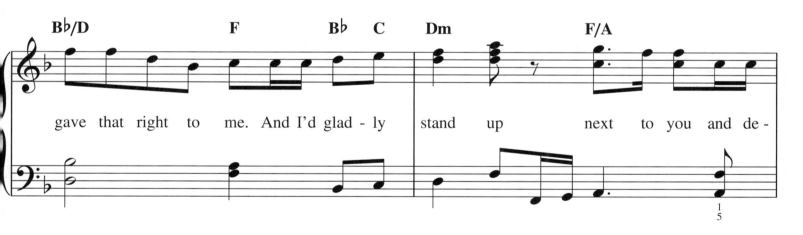

gave that right to me. And I'd glad-ly stand up next to you and de-

To Coda ⊕

fend her still to-day, 'cause there ain't no doubt I love this land,___

God bless the U. S. A.

From the lakes of Min - ne - so - ta to the

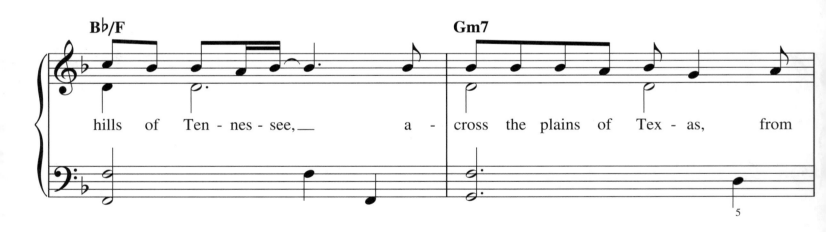

hills of Ten - nes - see,___ a - cross the plains of Tex - as, from

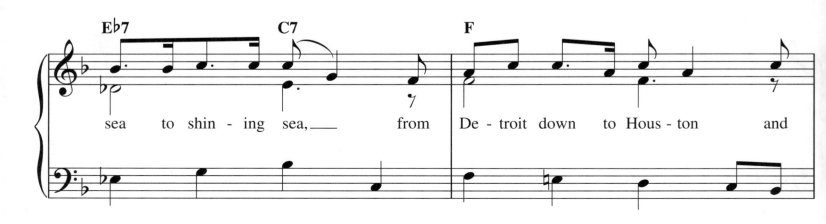

sea to shin - ing sea,___ from De - troit down to Hous - ton and

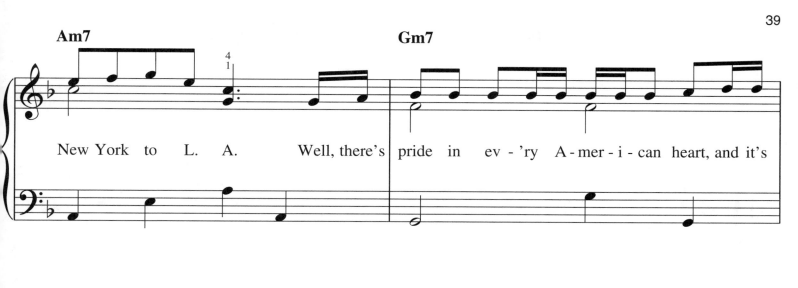

New York to L. A. Well, there's pride in ev-'ry A-mer-i-can heart, and it's

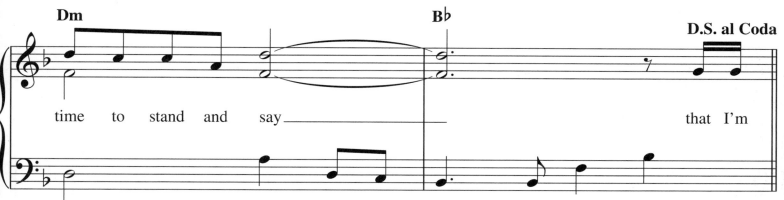

time to stand and say _____ that I'm

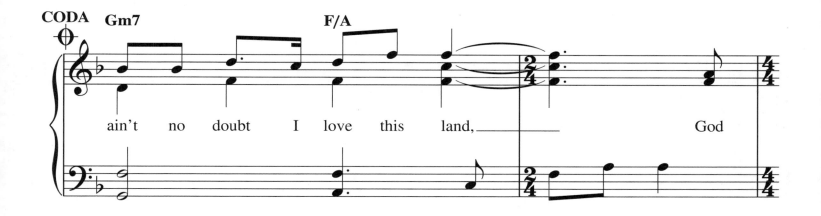

ain't no doubt I love this land, _____ God

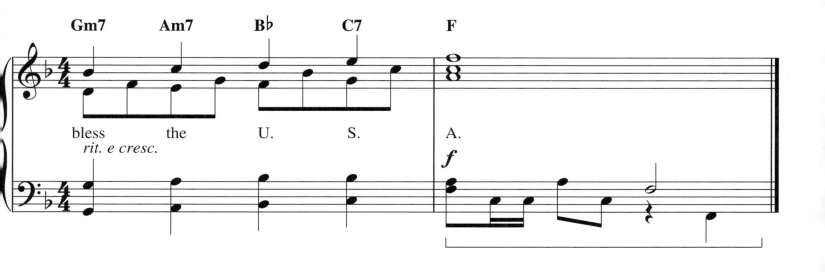

bless the U. S. A.

rit. e cresc.

f

I BELIEVE I CAN FLY

from SPACE JAM

Words and Music by
ROBERT KELLY

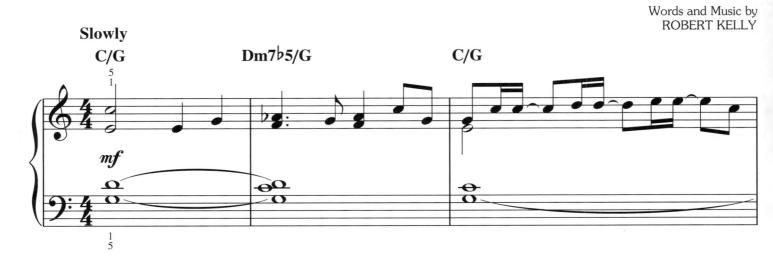

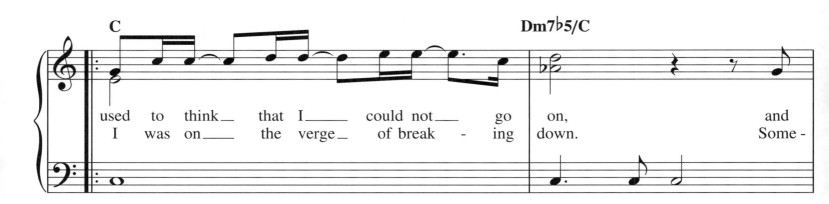

used to think__ that I__ could not__ go on, and
I was on__ the verge__ of break - ing down. Some -

life was noth - ing but__ an aw - ful song.__ But
times si - lence__ can seem__ so loud.__ There are

now I know_ the mean - ing of___ true | love._____ I'm
mir - a - cles___ in life___ I must_ a - | chieve,_____ but

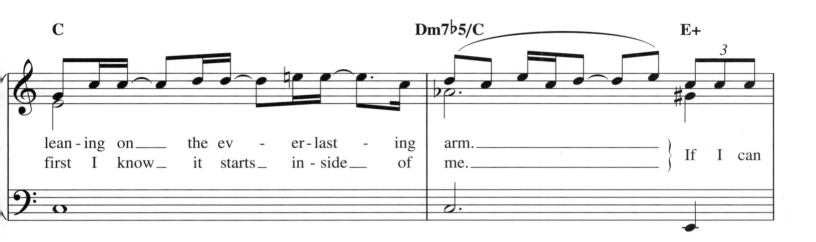

lean - ing on_____ the ev - er-last - ing | arm._____ If I can
first I know_ it starts_ in - side_ of | me._____ If I can

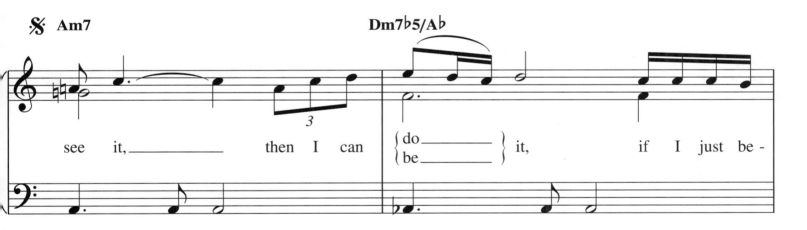

see it,_____ then I can | do_____ it, if I just be -
| be_____

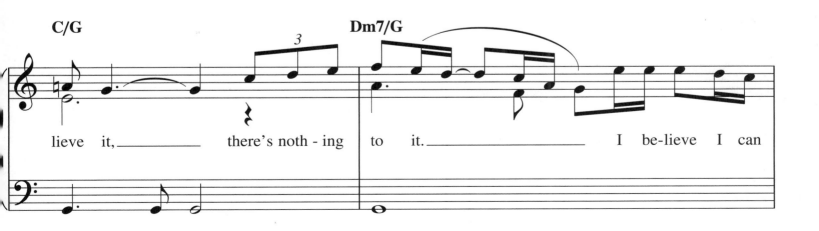

lieve it,_____ there's noth - ing | to it._____ I be-lieve I can

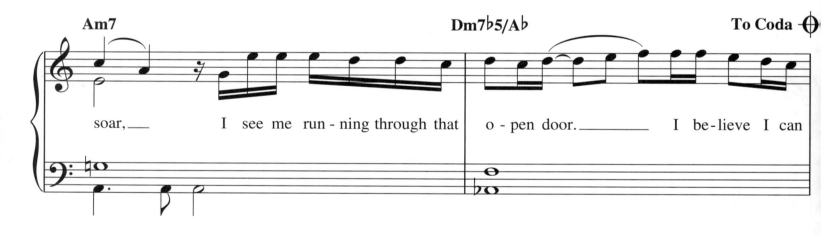

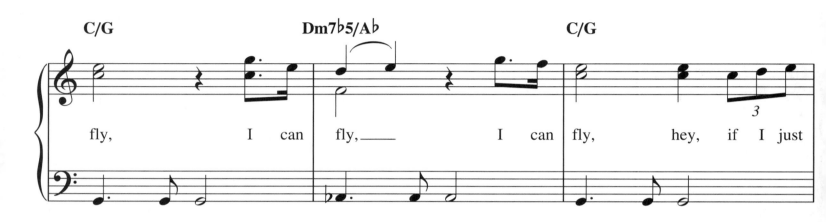

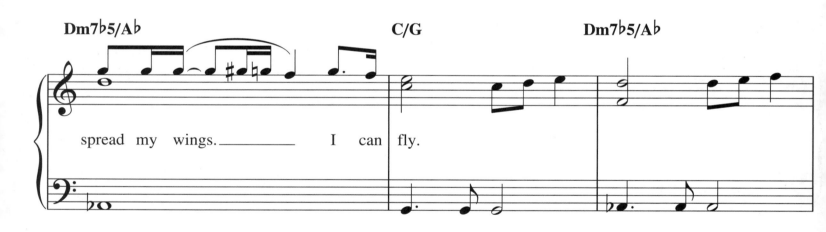

I HOPE YOU DANCE

Words and Music by TIA SILLERS
and MARK D. SANDERS

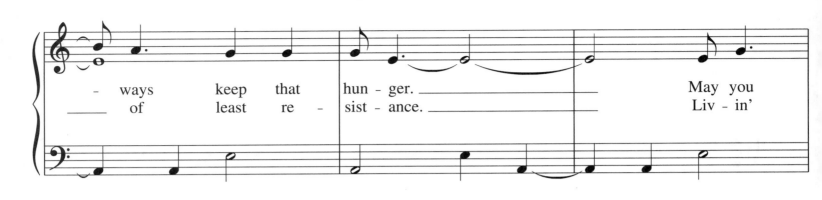

- ways   keep   that   hun - ger. _____   May you
____ of   least   re -   sist - ance. _____   Liv - in'

F

nev - er   take __ one   sin - gle   breath __ for grant   - ed. _____
might mean   tak - in'   chanc - es   if they're   worth tak   - in'. _____

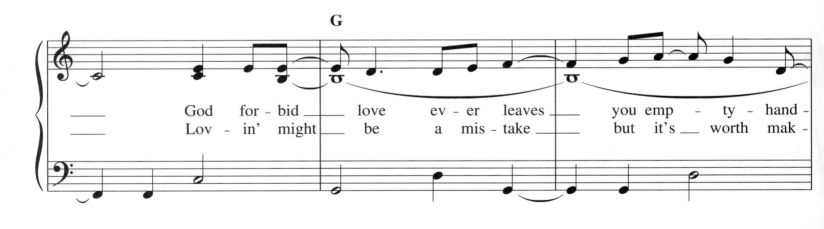

G

____ God   for - bid __   love   ev - er   leaves ____   you emp - ty - hand-
____ Lov - in' might __   be   a   mis - take ____   but it's __ worth mak-

F   **G**

- ed. _____   I hope you   still __   feel   small __   when you
- in'. _____   Don't   let __   some   hell -   bent

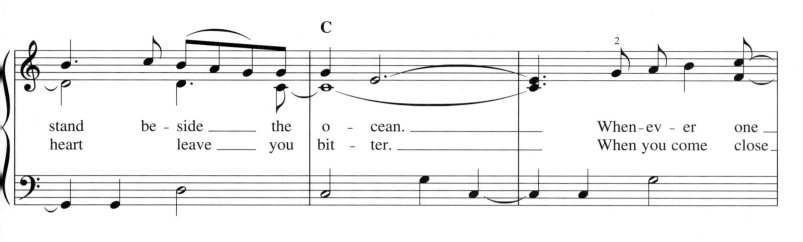

stand   be - side _____ the   o - cean. _____   When-ev - er   one __
heart   leave _____ you   bit - ter. _____   When you come   close __

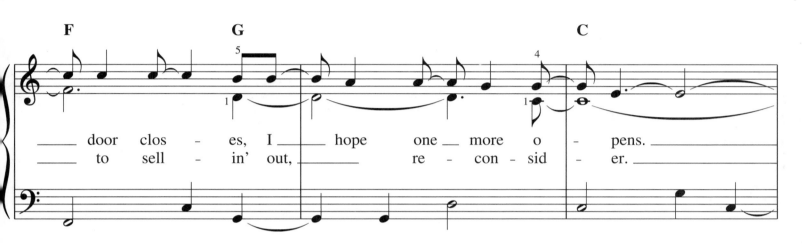

_____ door   clos - es, I _____ hope   one __ more   o - pens. _____
_____ to   sell - in' out, _____   re - con - sid - er. _____

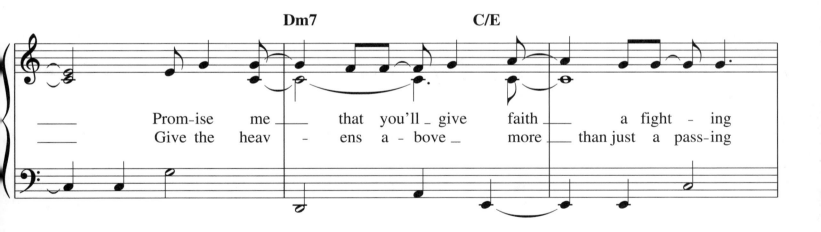

_____ Prom-ise   me _____ that   you'll _ give   faith _____ a   fight - ing
_____ Give the   heav - ens a - bove _ more _____ than just   a   pass-ing

To Coda ⊕

chance. _____
glance. _____   And when you | get the choice   to | sit it out   or

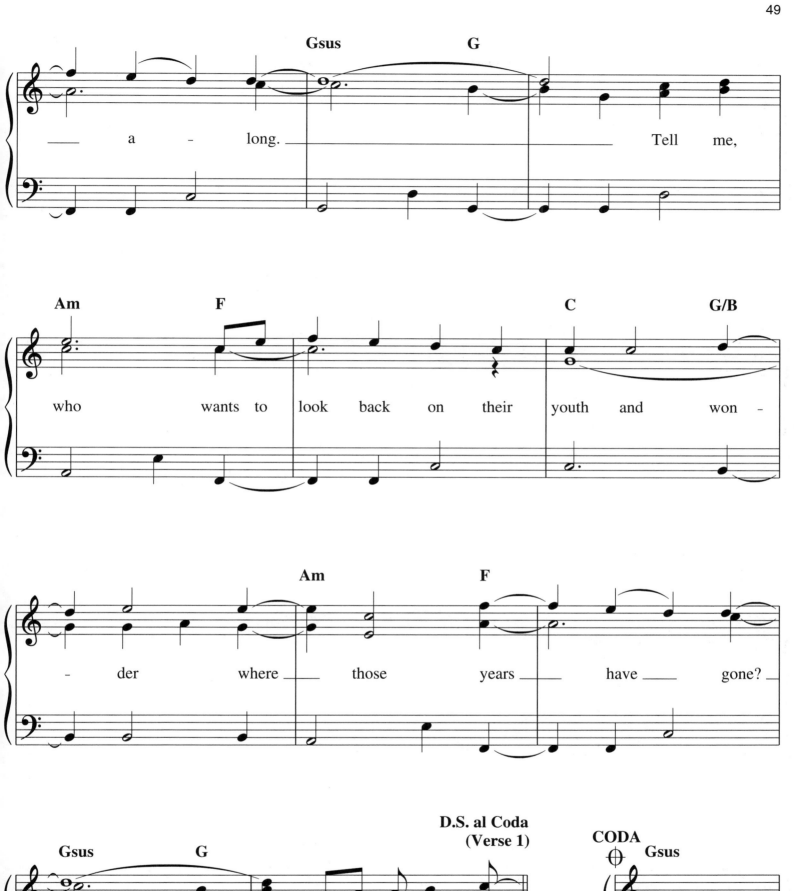

a - long. _____ Tell me,

who _____ wants to look back on their youth and won -

- der where _____ those years _____ have _____ gone?

D.S. al Coda
(Verse 1)

CODA

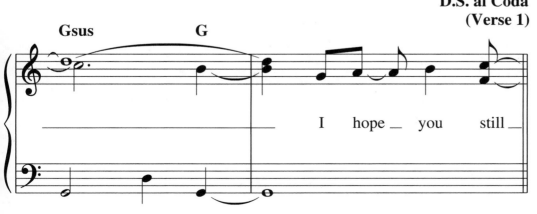

I hope _____ you still _____

dance.

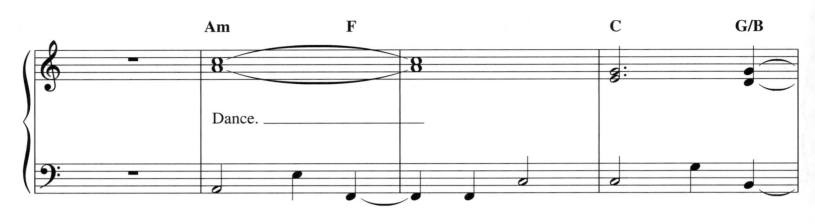

Am **F** **C** **G/B**

Dance. _____

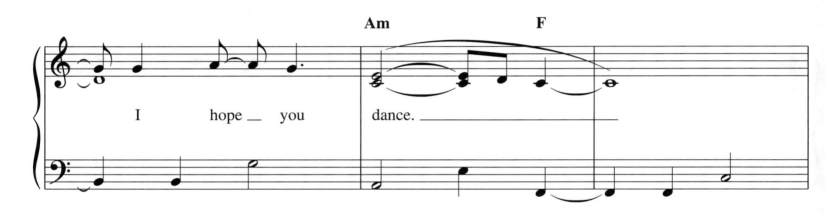

Am **F**

I hope __ you dance. _____

Gsus **G** **Am** **F**

I hope __ you dance. __ Time is a

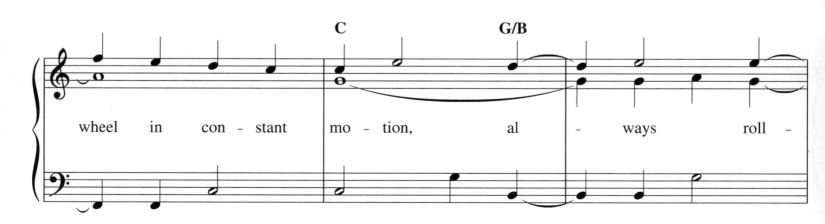

C **G/B**

wheel in con - stant mo - tion, al - ways roll -

I'M ALREADY THERE

Words and Music by GARY BAKER,
FRANK MYERS and RICHIE McDONALD

hear her say___ "I love___ you" one___ more time.___

And when he heard___ the sound___ of the

kids laugh - in' in the back - ground,___ he had to wipe a - way___ a tear___

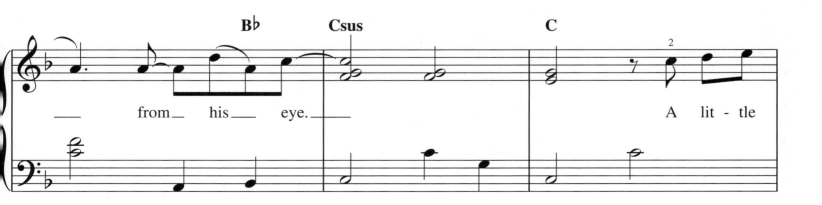

___ from___ his___ eye.___ A lit - tle

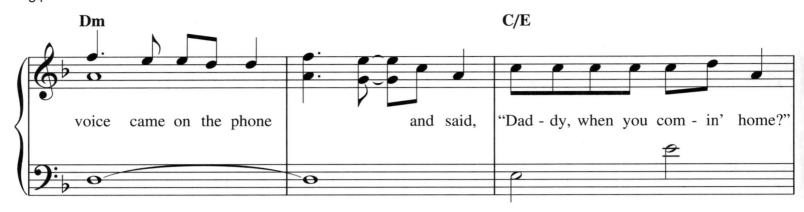

Dm ... **C/E**

voice came on the phone and said, "Dad - dy, when you com - in' home?"

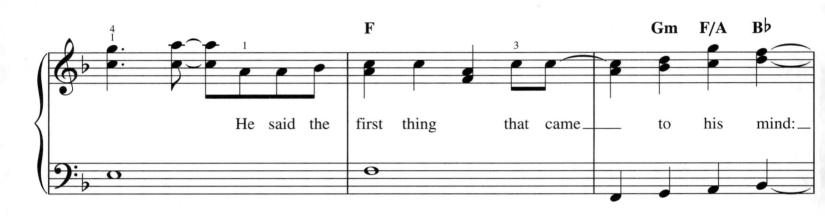

F ... **Gm** **F/A** **B♭**

He said the first thing that came to his mind:

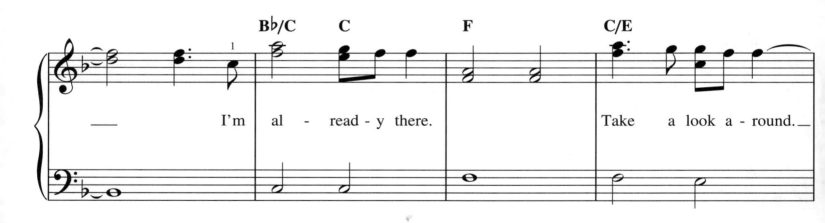

B♭/C **C** ... **F** ... **C/E**

I'm al - read - y there. Take a look a - round.

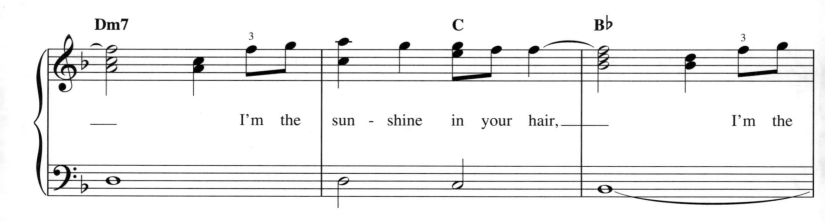

Dm7 ... **C** ... **B♭**

I'm the sun - shine in your hair, I'm the

shad - ow on the ground.___ I'm the whis - per in the wind,___

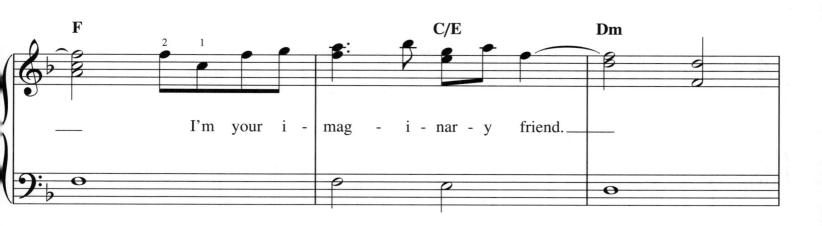

___ I'm your i - mag - i - nar - y friend.___

And I know___ I'm in your prayers.___ Oh, I'm

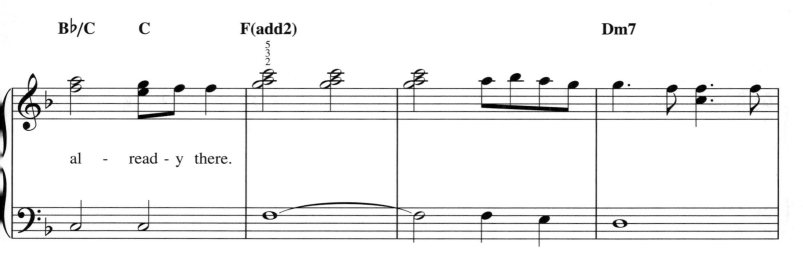

al - read - y there.

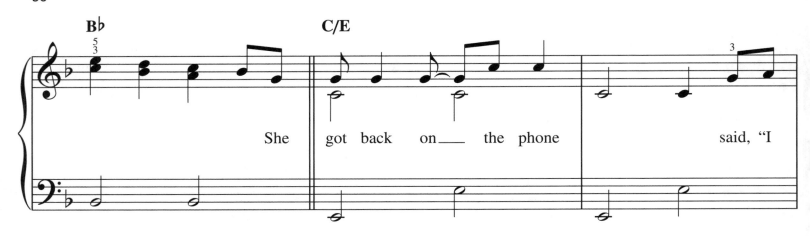

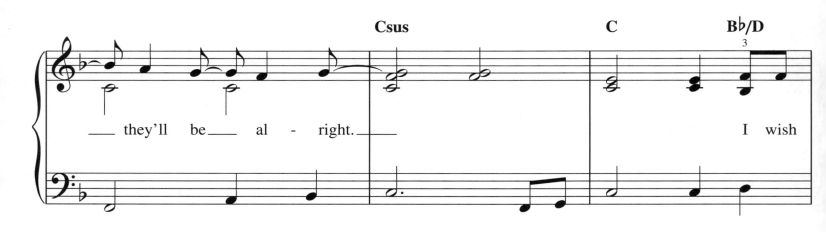

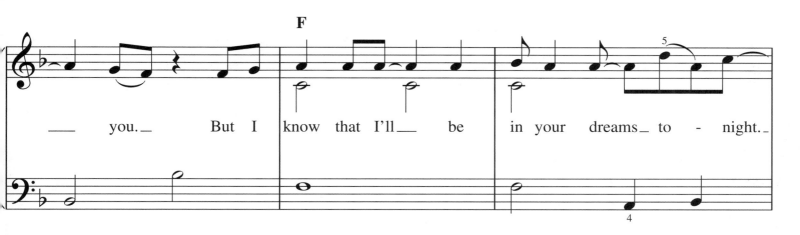

_____ you._____ But I know that I'll_____ be in your dreams_ to - night._

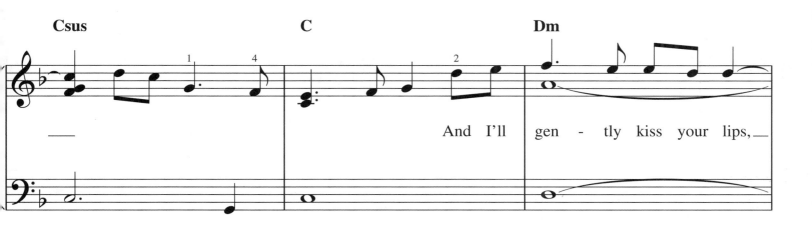

_____ And I'll gen - tly kiss your lips,_____

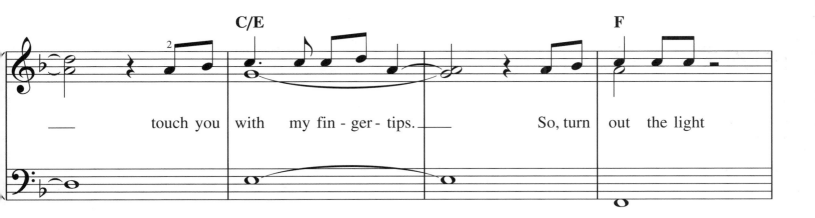

_____ touch you with my fin - ger - tips._____ So, turn out the light

and close your eyes._____ I'm al - read - y there._____

Don't make a sound____ I'm the beat of your heart,____ I'm the

moon - light shin - in' down.____ I'm the whis - per in the wind,____

____ and I'll be there till the end.____

Can you feel____ the love that we've shared?____ Oh, I'm

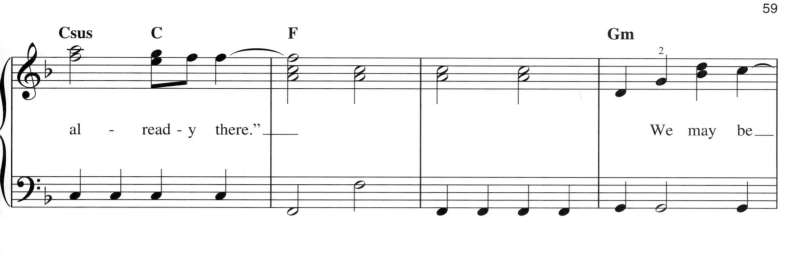

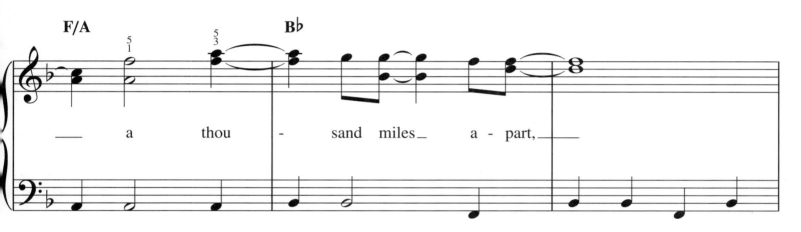

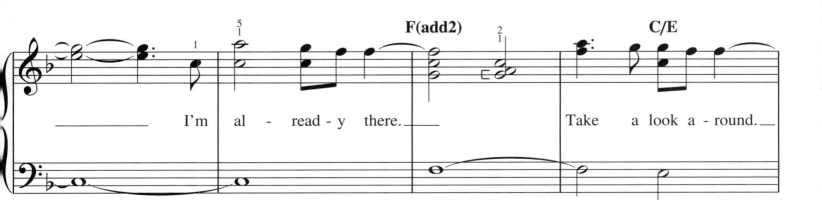

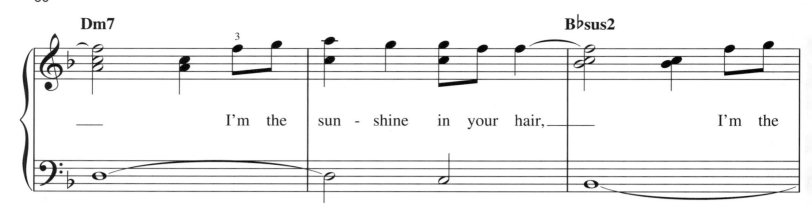

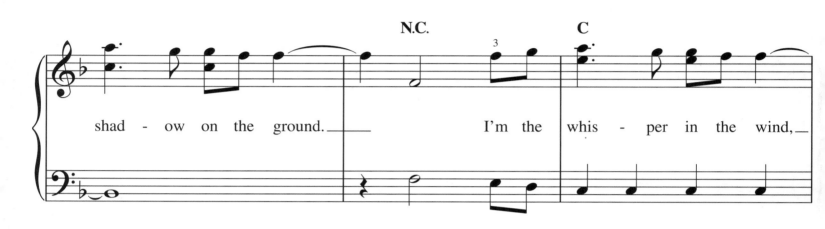

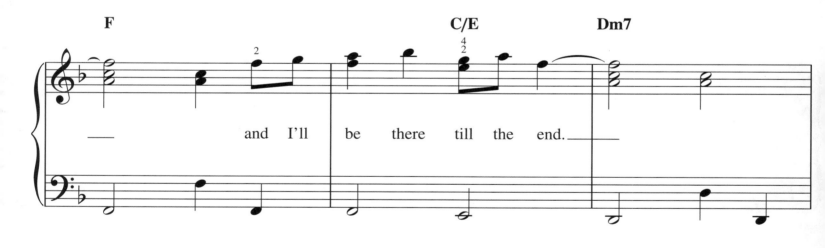

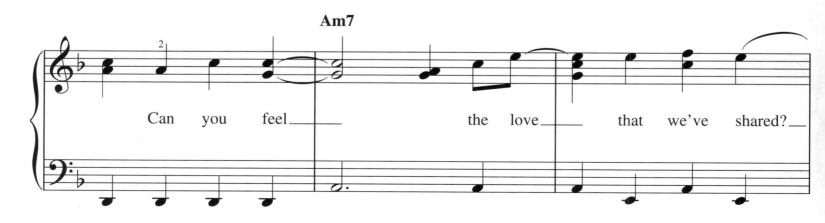

Oh, I'm al - read - y there.

Yeah, oh, I'm al - read - y there.

JESUS TAKE THE WHEEL

Words and Music by BRETT JAMES,
GORDIE SAMPSON and HILLARY LINDSEY

63

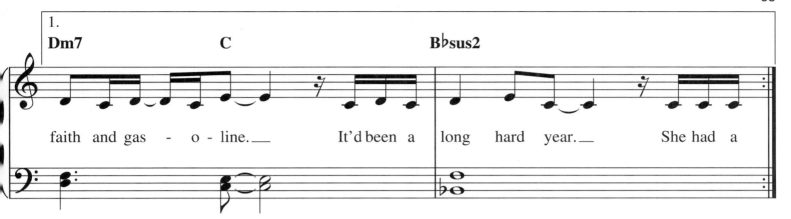

faith and gas - o - line.___ It'd been a long hard year.___ She had a

She did-n't e - ven have time to cry.___ She was so scared.___ She threw her

hands up in___ the air:___ "Je - sus, take___ the wheel;___

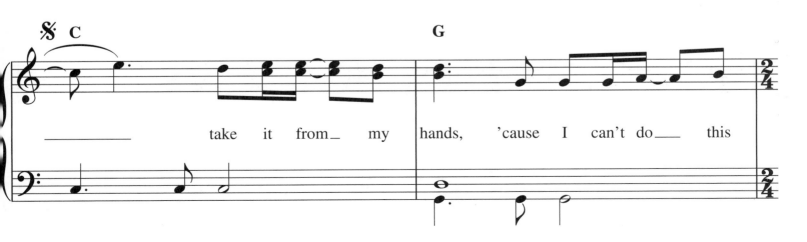

_____ take it from___ my hands, 'cause I can't do___ this

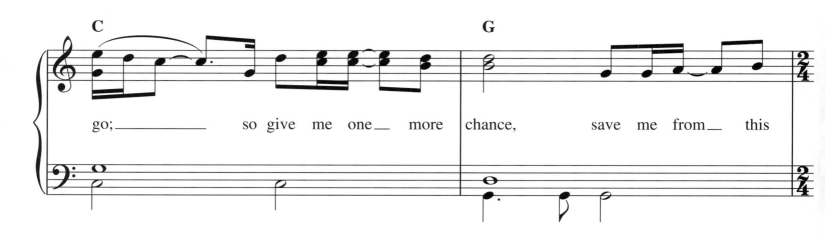

It was | still get-ting cold-er when she made it to the shoul-der and the

car came to a stop:__ and she | cried when she saw that ba - by in the back seat

sleep-ing like_ a rock._ And for the | first time_ in a long___ time, she

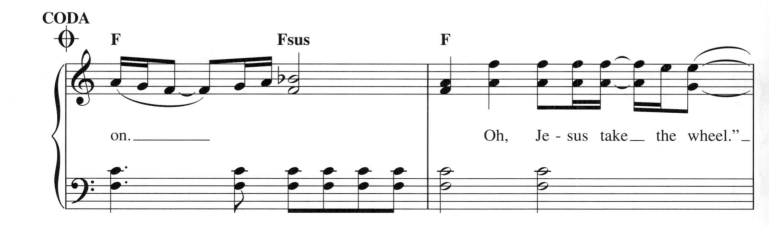

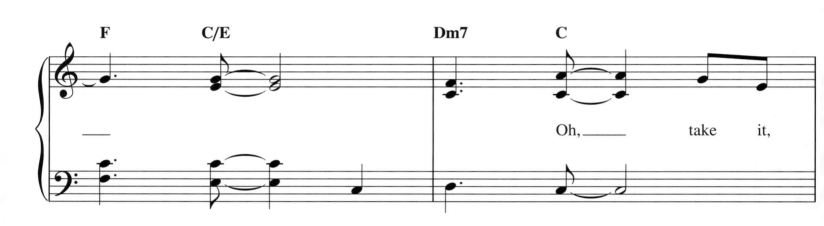

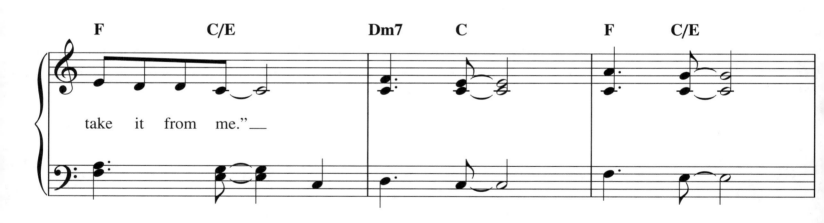

ONLY HOPE

from the Warner Bros. Motion Picture A WALK TO REMEMBER

Words and Music by
JONATHAN FOREMAN

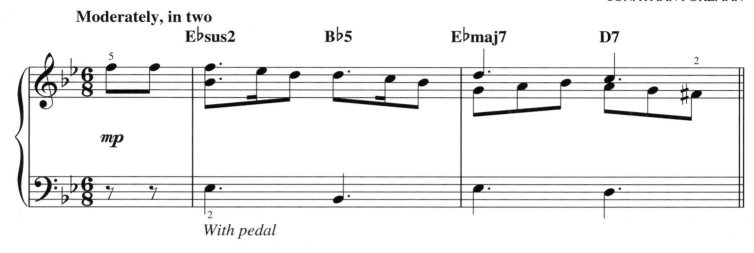

With pedal

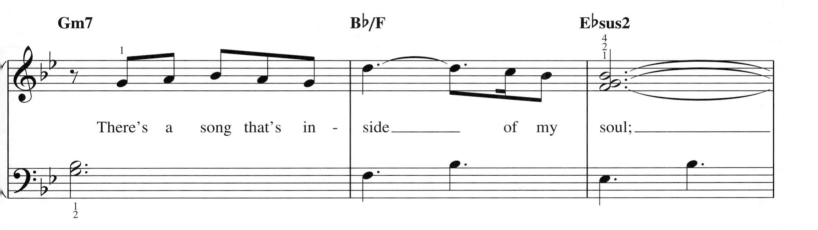

There's a song that's in - side____ of my soul;____

____ it's the one that I've tried____ to write

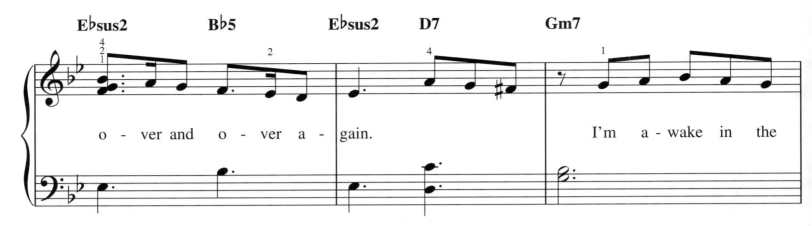

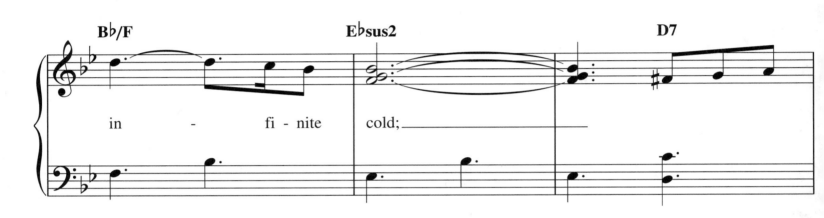

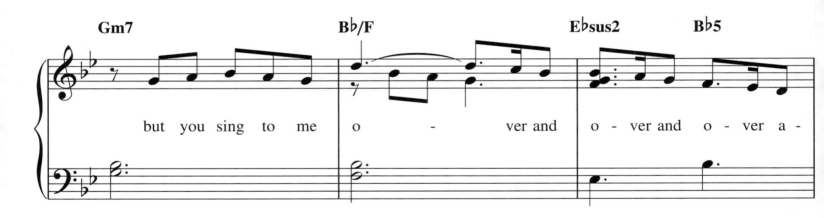

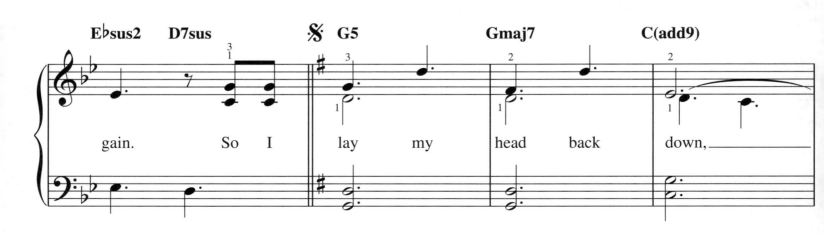

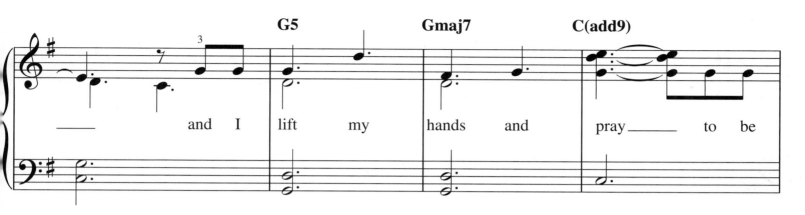

G5   Gmaj7   C(add9)

and   I   lift   my   hands   and   pray_____ to be

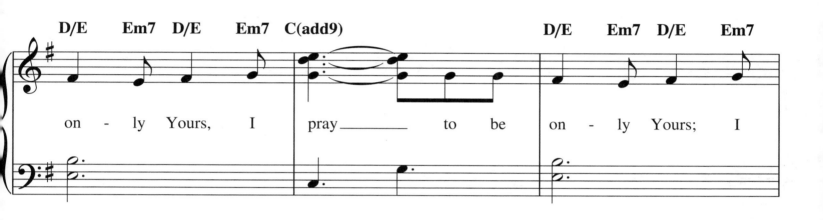

D/E   Em7 D/E   Em7 C(add9)   D/E   Em7 D/E   Em7

on - ly Yours,   I   pray_____ to   be   on - ly Yours;   I

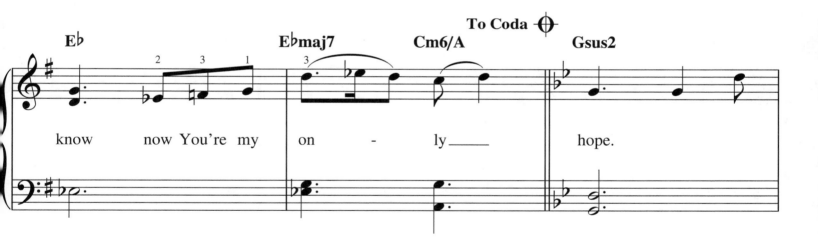

To Coda ⊕

Eb   Ebmaj7   Cm6/A   Gsus2

know   now You're my   on - ly_____   hope.

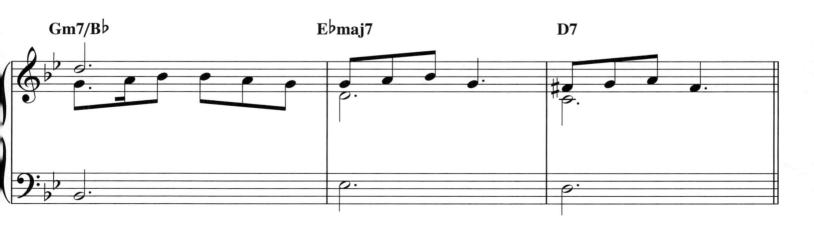

Gm7/Bb   Ebmaj7   D7

Sing to me___ the song___ of the stars,___
When it feels like my dreams___ are so far,___

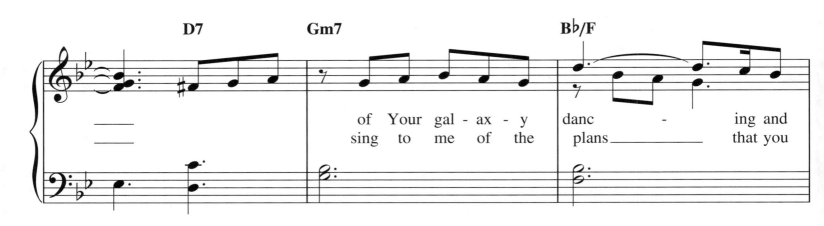

___ of Your gal - ax - y danc - ing and
___ sing to me of the plans___ that you

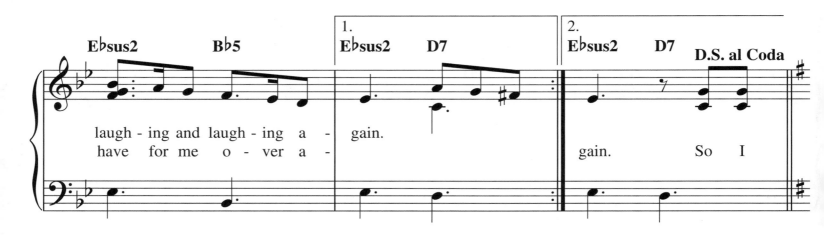

laugh - ing and laugh - ing a - gain.
have for me o - ver a - gain. So I

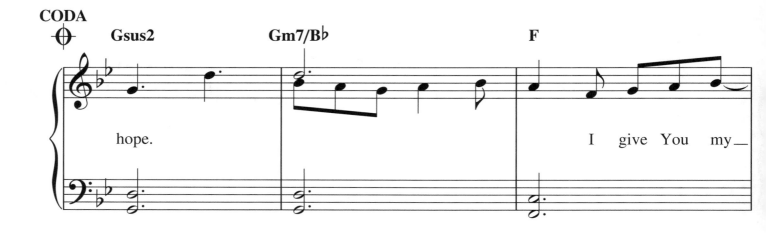

CODA

hope.

I give You my___

des - ti - ny. I'm giv - ing You all of me.

I want Your sym - pho - ny sing - ing in all that I

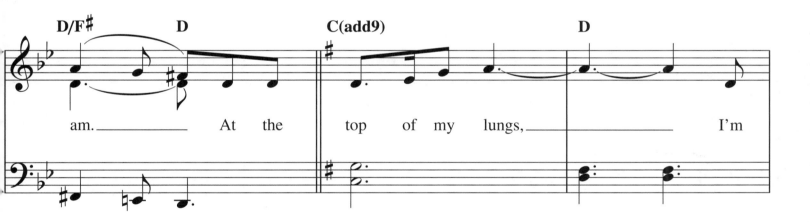

am. At the top of my lungs, I'm

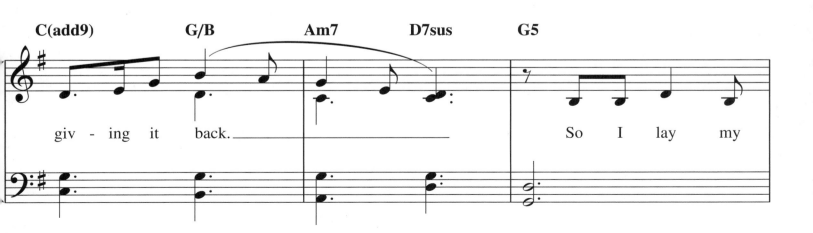

giv - ing it back. So I lay my

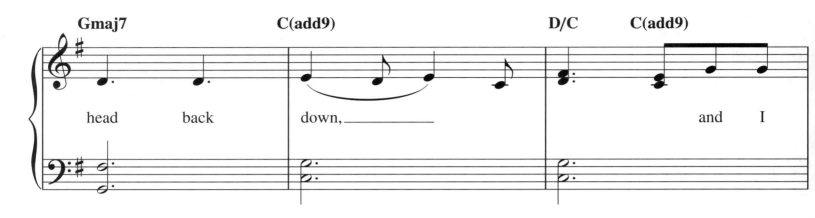

head   back   down,_____   and   I

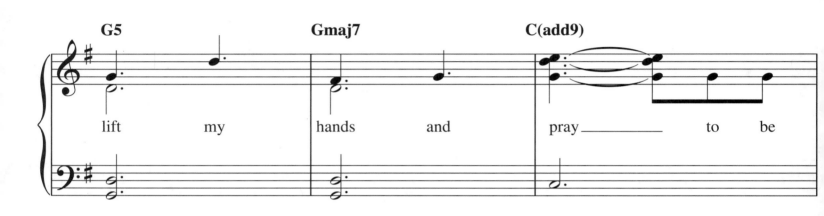

lift   my   hands   and   pray_____   to   be

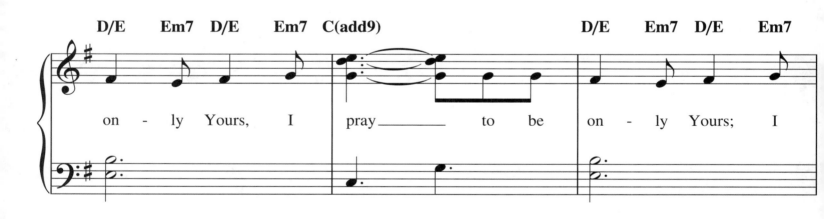

on - ly Yours, I   pray_____   to   be   on - ly Yours;   I

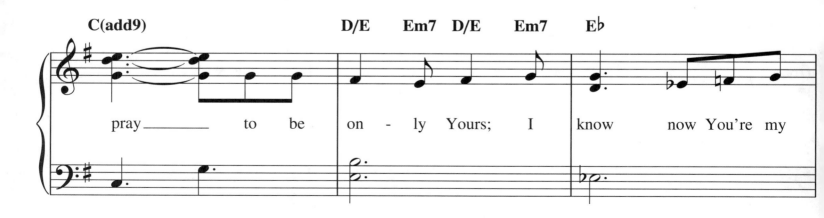

pray_____   to   be   on - ly Yours;   I   know   now You're my

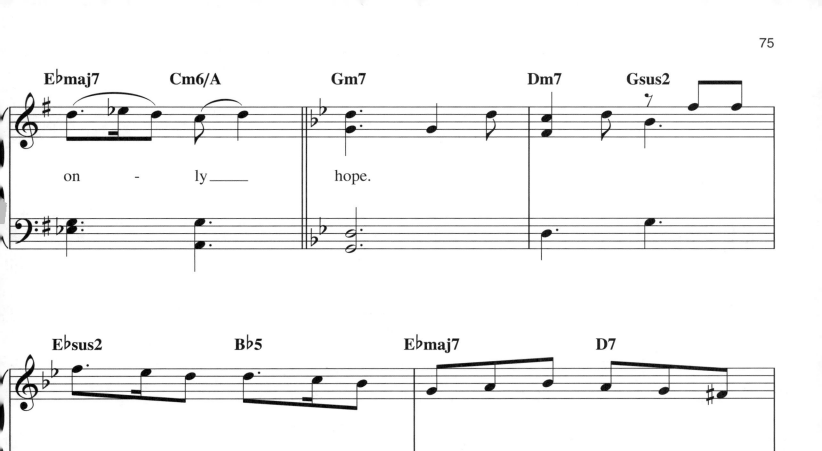

on - ly____ hope.

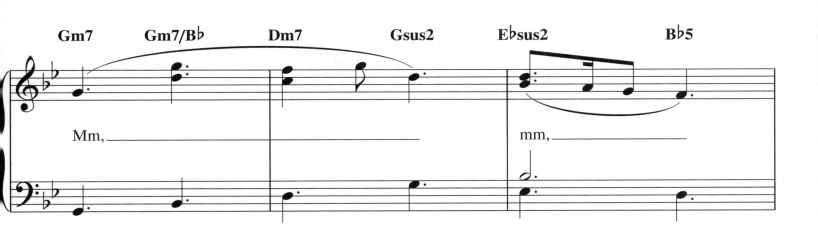

Mm,_____ mm,_____

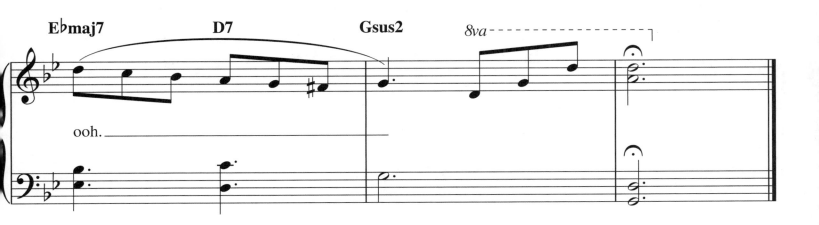

ooh._____

A MOMENT LIKE THIS

Words and Music by JOHN REID
and JORGEN KJELL ELOFSSON

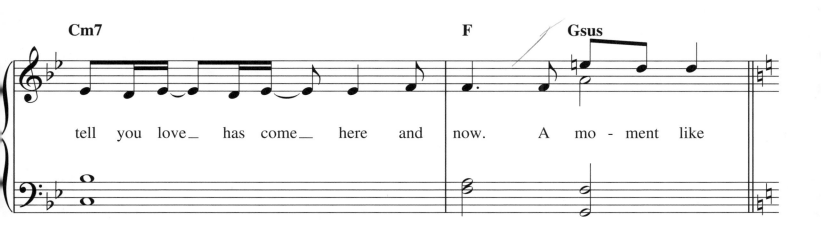

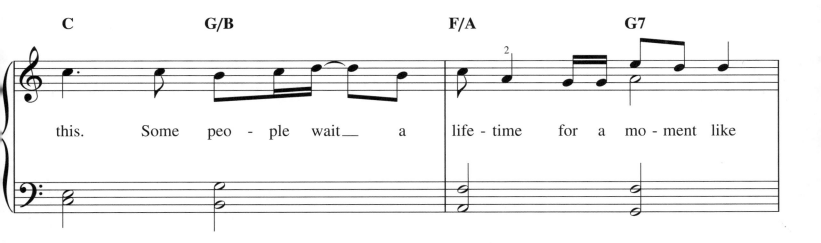

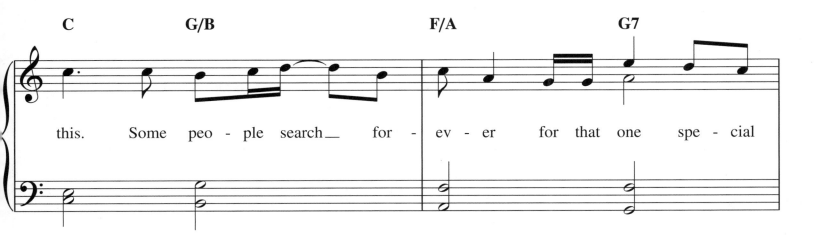

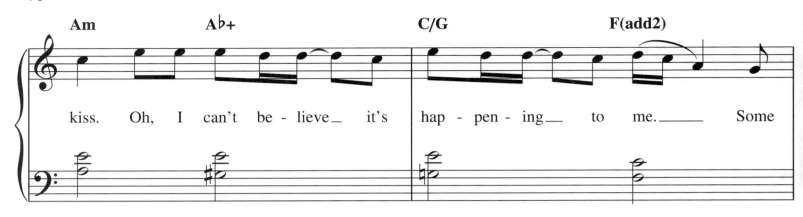

kiss. Oh, I can't be - lieve___ it's hap - pen - ing___ to me.___ Some

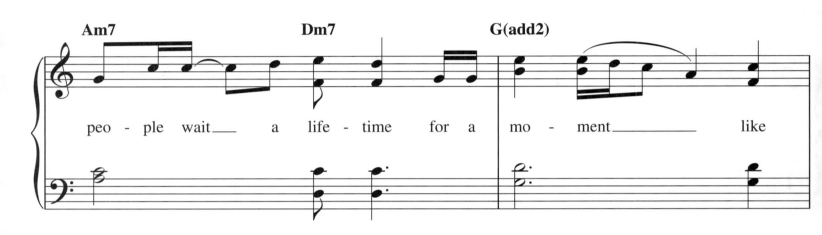

peo - ple wait___ a life - time for a mo - ment_____ like

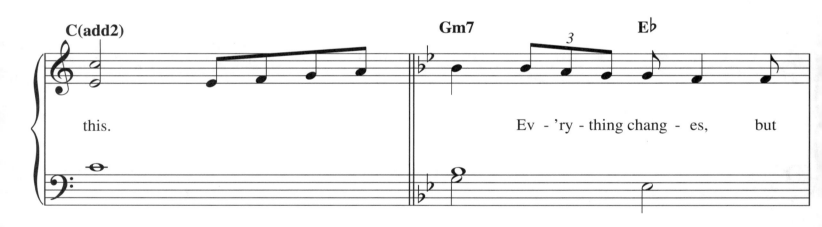

this. Ev - 'ry - thing chang - es, but

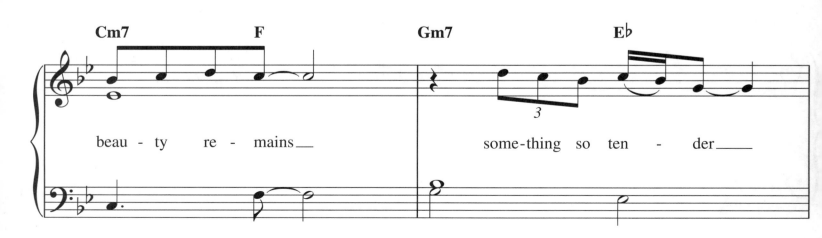

beau - ty re - mains___ some - thing so ten - der___

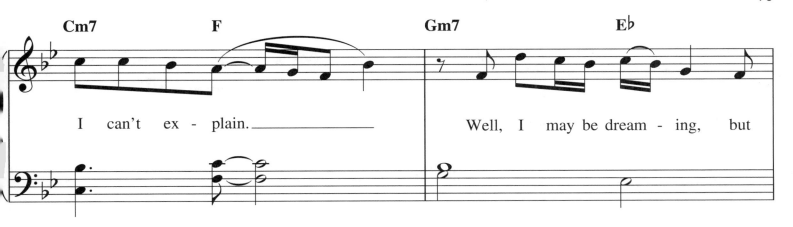

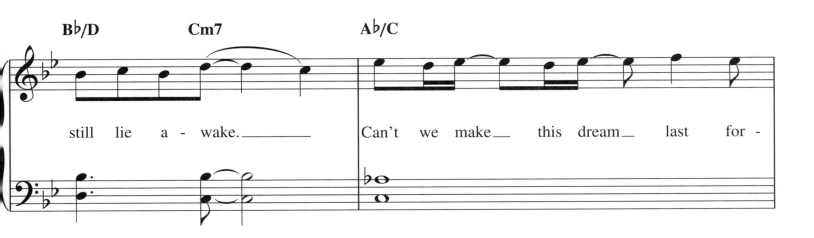

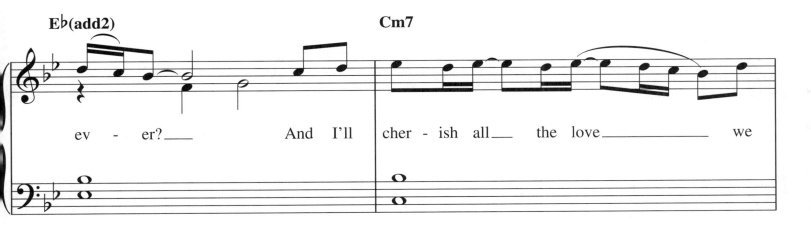

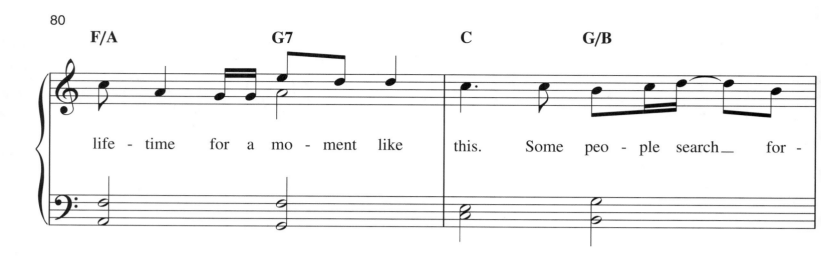

life - time for a mo - ment like this. Some peo - ple search for -

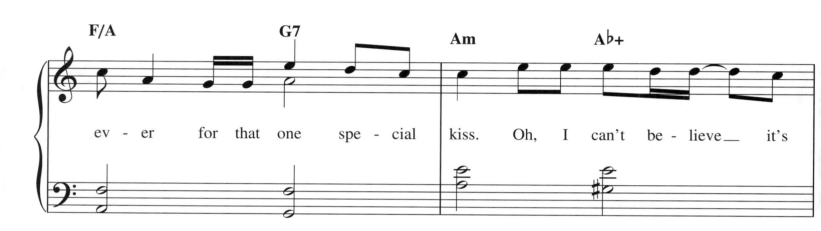

ev - er for that one spe - cial kiss. Oh, I can't be - lieve it's

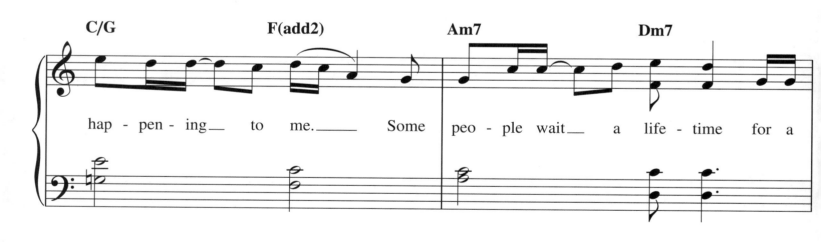

hap - pen - ing to me. Some peo - ple wait a life - time for a

mo - ment like this. Could this be the great - est love of

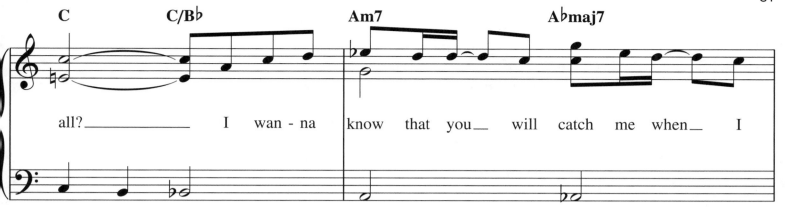

all?_____ I wan - na know that you_ will catch me when_ I

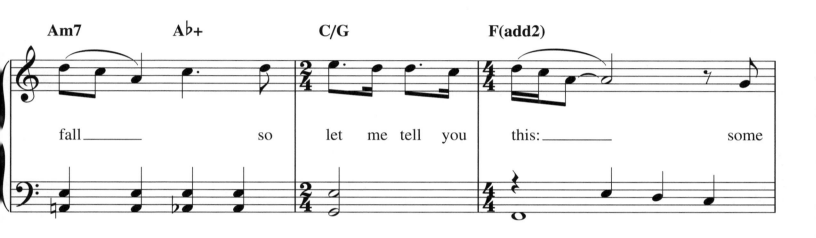

fall_____ so let me tell you this:_____ some

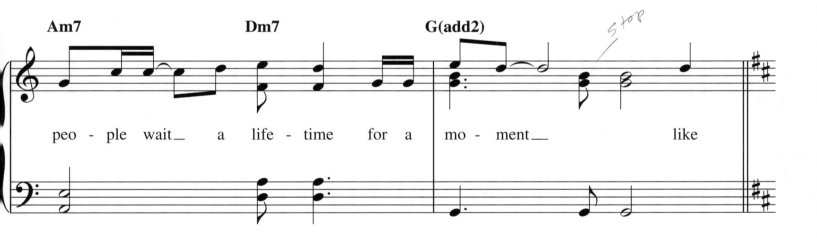

peo - ple wait_ a life - time for a mo - ment_ like

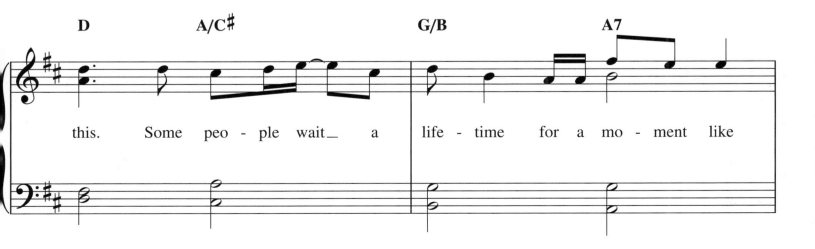

this. Some peo - ple wait_ a life - time for a mo - ment like

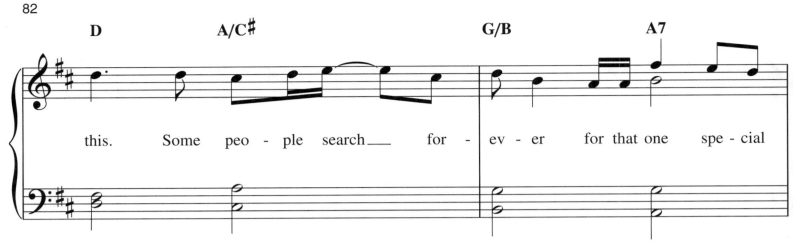

this. Some peo - ple search___ for - ev - er for that one spe - cial

kiss. Oh, I can't be - lieve___ it's hap - pen - ing___ to me.___ Some

peo - ple wait___ a life - time for a mo - ment___ like

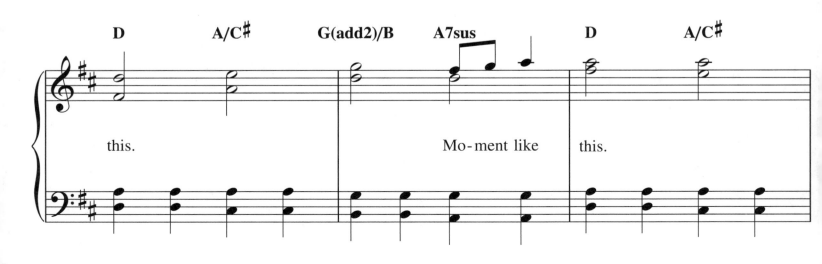

this. Mo - ment like this.

MY HEART WILL GO ON

(Love Theme from 'Titanic')
from the Paramount and Twentieth Century Fox Motion Picture TITANIC

Music by JAMES HORNER
Lyric by WILL JENNINGS

With pedal

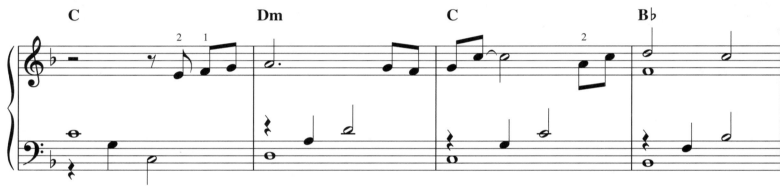

Ev - 'ry night in my dreams I see you, I

feel you, that is how I know you go on. ____

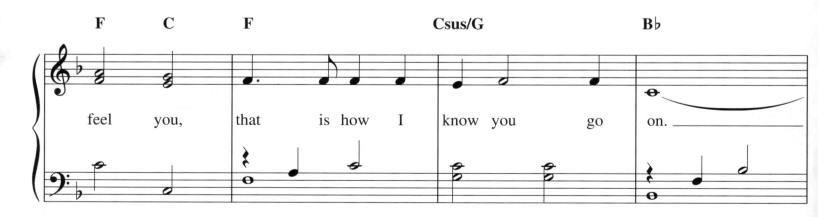

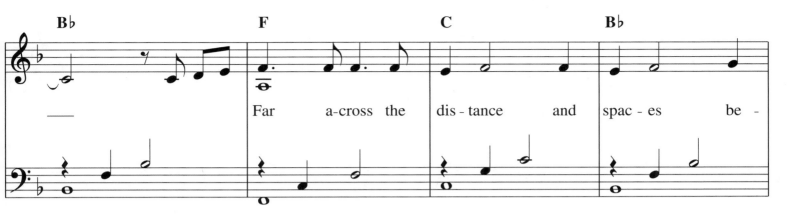

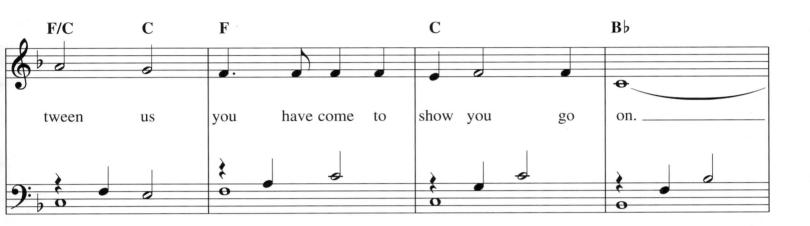

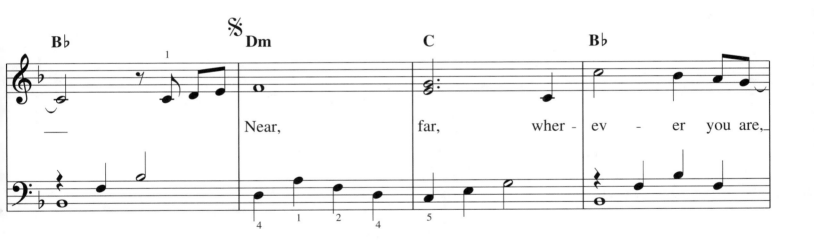

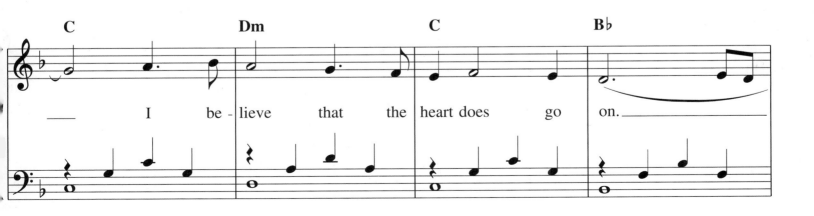

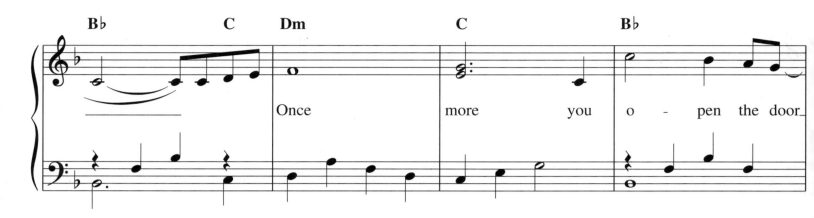

Once more you o - pen the door

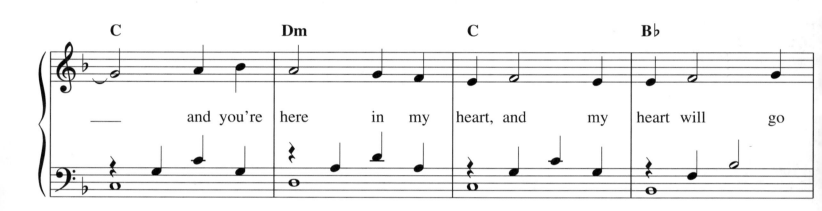

and you're here in my heart, and my heart will go

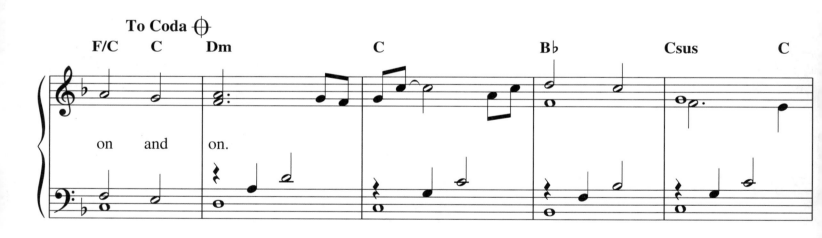

To Coda ⊕

on and on.

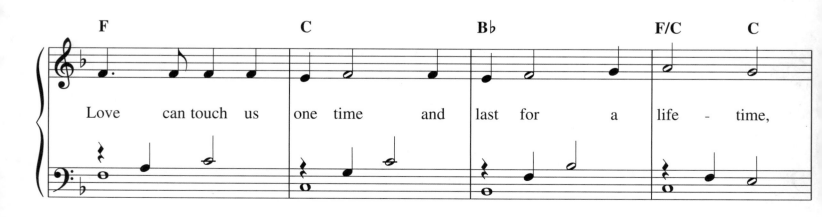

Love can touch us one time and last for a life - time,

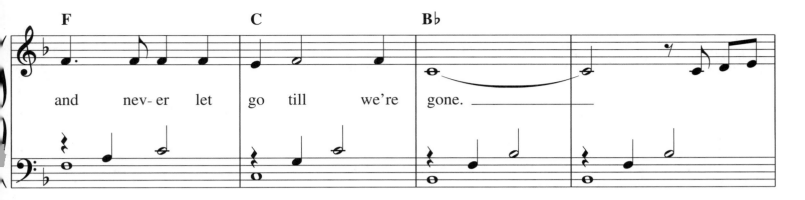

and nev-er let go till we're gone.

Love was when I loved you; one true time I hold to.

D.S. al Coda

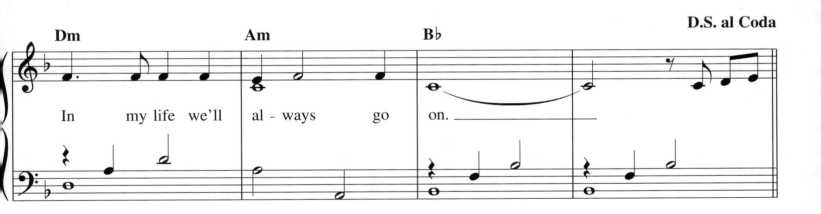

In my life we'll al-ways go on.

CODA

on.

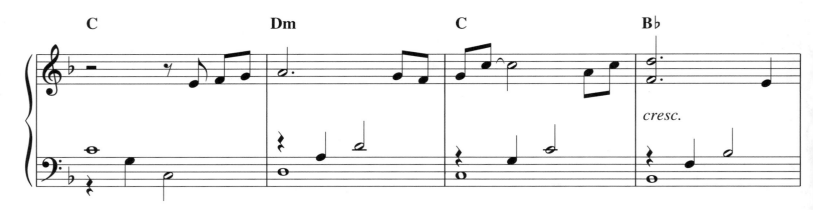

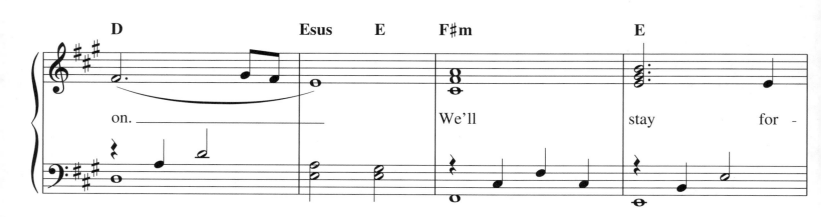

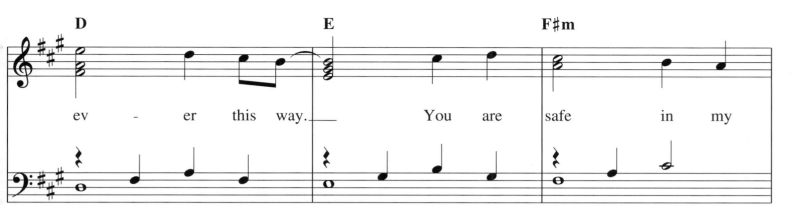

ev - er this way.___ You are safe in my

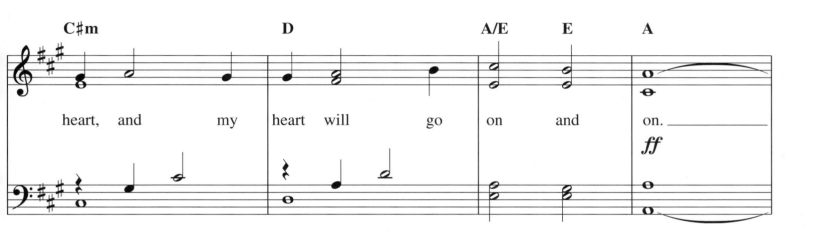

heart, and my heart will go on and on.___

ff

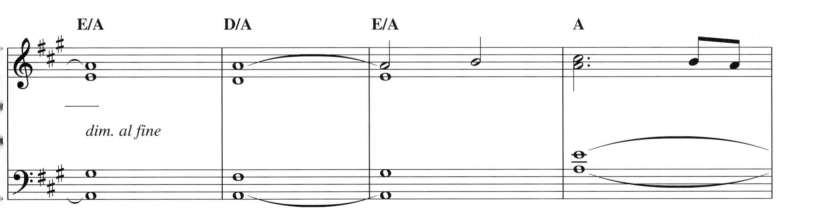

dim. al fine

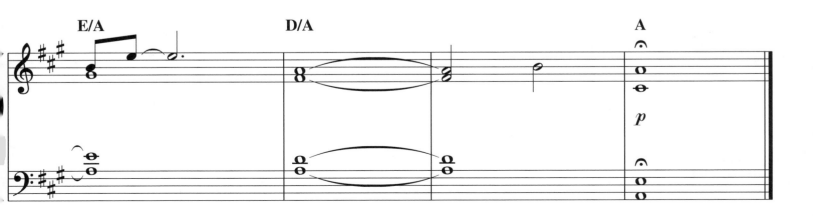

p

SOMEWHERE OUT THERE

from AN AMERICAN TAIL

Music by BARRY MANN and JAMES HORNER
Lyric by CYNTHIA WEIL

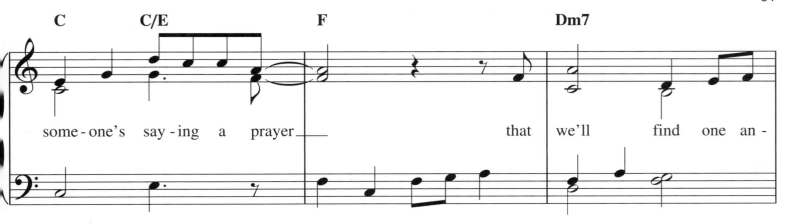

some-one's say-ing a prayer____ that we'll find one an-

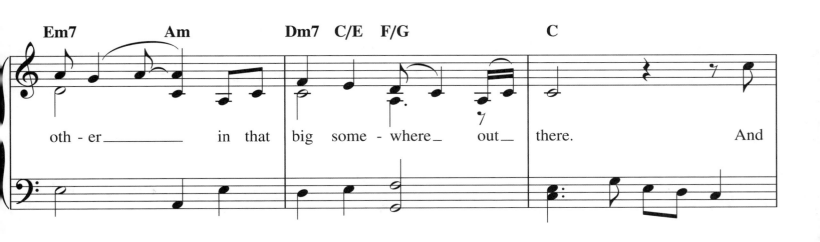

oth - er_____ in that big some - where__ out__ there. And

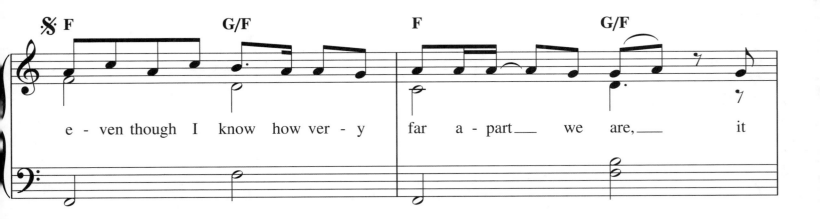

e - ven though I know how ver - y far a - part__ we are,__ it

helps to think__ we might be wish - in' on the same__ bright star. And

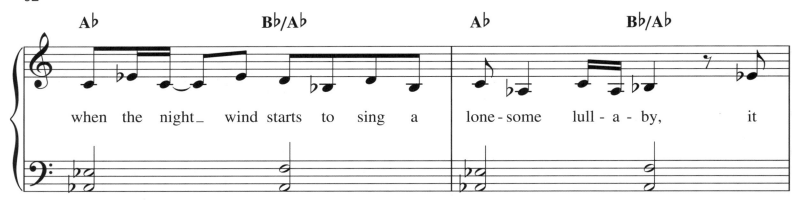

when the night__ wind starts to sing a lone-some lull-a-by, it

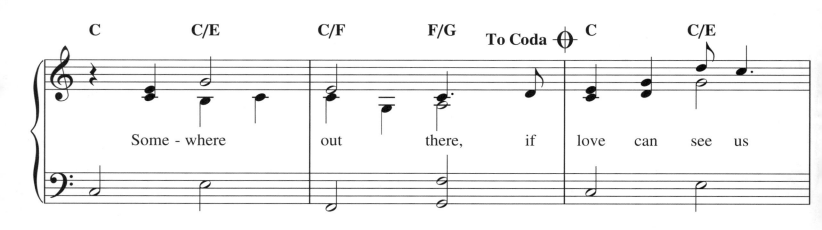

helps to think we're sleep-ing un-der -neath the same big sky.

poco rit. *a tempo*

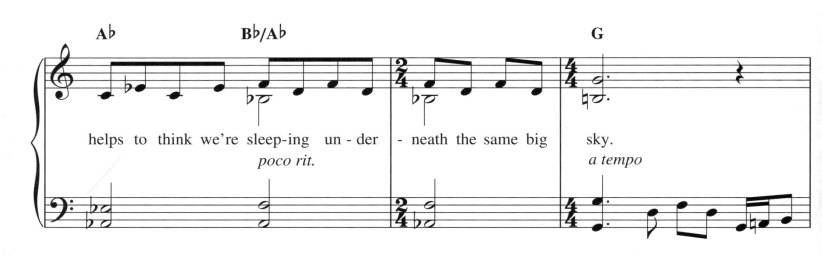

Some - where out there, if love can see us

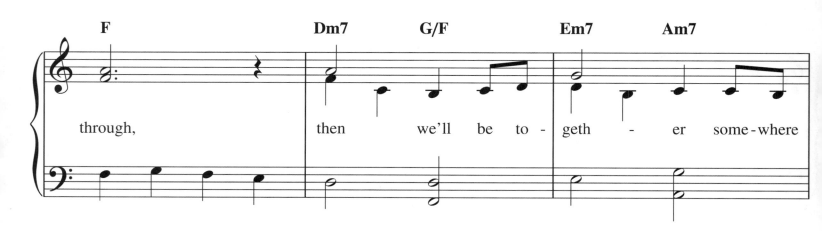

through, then we'll be to - geth - er some-where

D.S. al Coda

out there,   out   where dreams   come   true._____   And

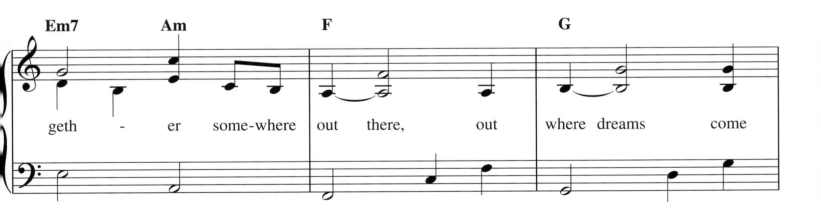

love can see us   through,   then   we'll be to-

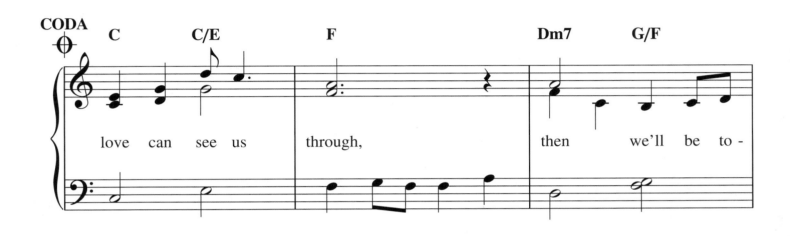

geth - er some-where out there,   out   where dreams   come

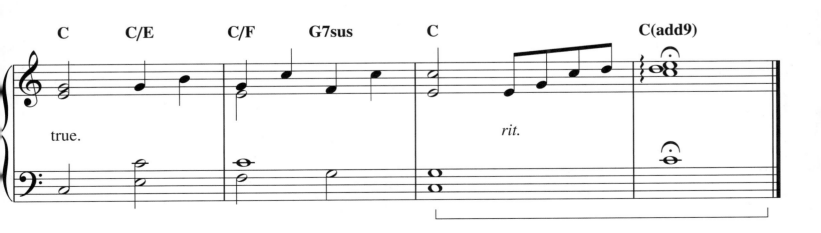

true.   rit.

UP TO THE MOUNTAIN
(MLK Song)

Words and Music by
PATTY GRIFFIN

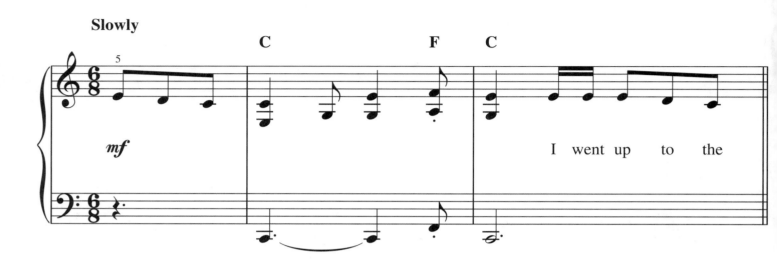

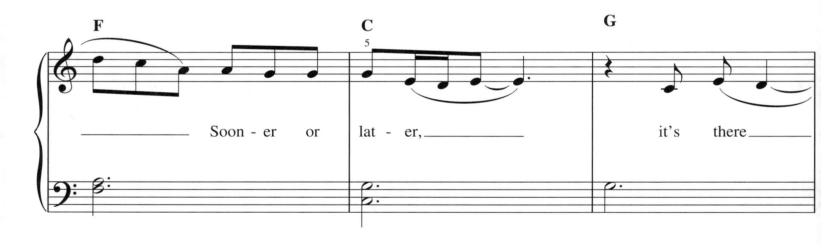

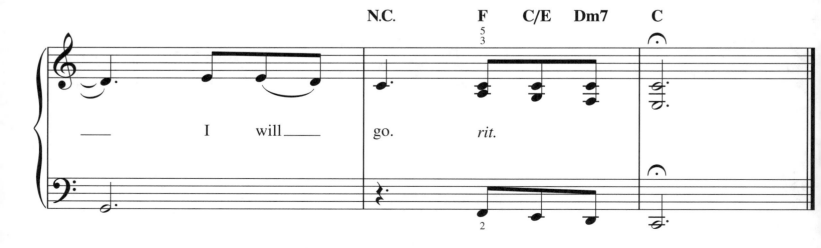

THAT'S WHAT LOVE IS FOR

Words and Music by MARK MUELLER,
MICHAEL OMARTIAN and AMY GRANT

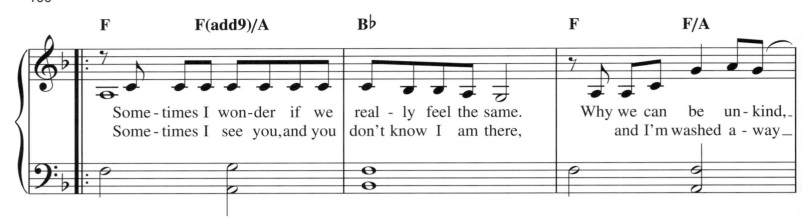

Some-times I won-der if we real-ly feel the same. Why we can be un-kind,
Some-times I see you, and you don't know I am there, and I'm washed a-way

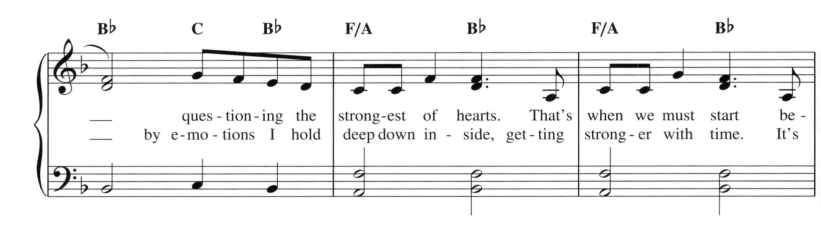

ques-tion-ing the strong-est of hearts. That's when we must start be-
by e-mo-tions I hold deep down in-side, get-ting strong-er with time. It's

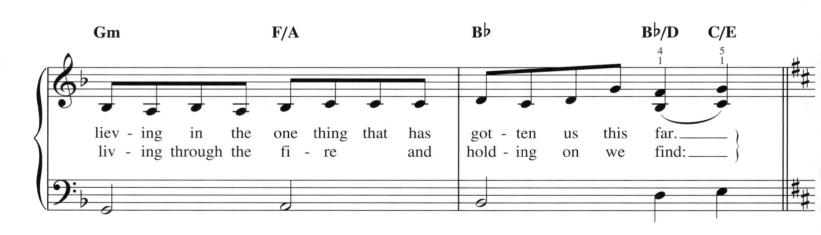

liev-ing in the one thing that has got-ten us this far.
liv-ing through the fi-re and hold-ing on we find:

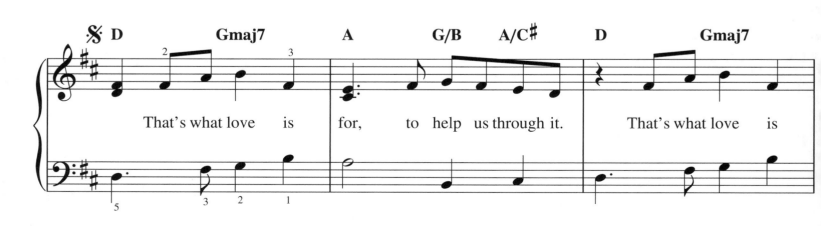

That's what love is for, to help us through it. That's what love is

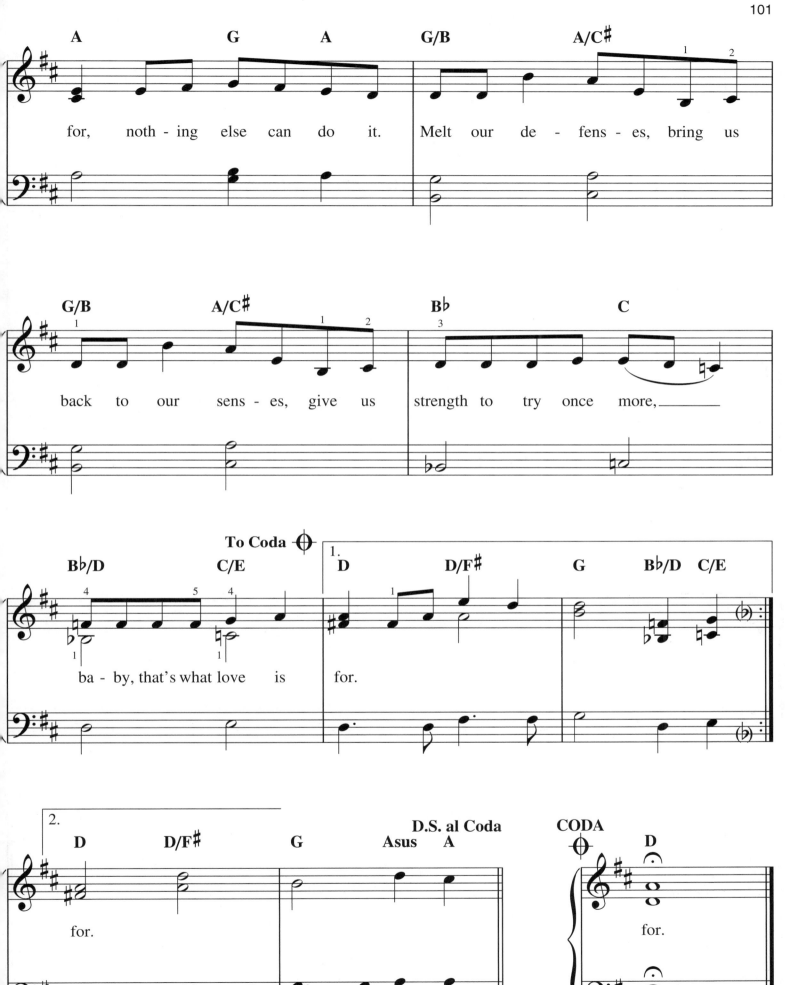

WAY UP THERE

Words and Music by
TENA CLARK

Slowly, with strength

With pedal

Way up there where peace re-mains, where

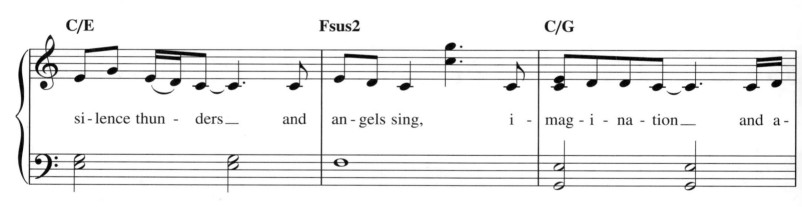

si-lence thun-ders___ and an-gels sing, i-mag-i-na-tion___ and a-

maz-ing grace bring us clos-er to our home___ in space. The
*(that per - fect place.)

Original lyrics

WHEN YOU BELIEVE

(From The Prince of Egypt)
from THE PRINCE OF EGYPT

Words and Music by STEPHEN SCHWARTZ
with Additional Music by BABYFACE

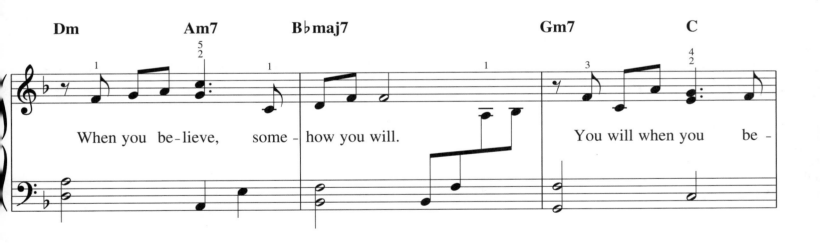

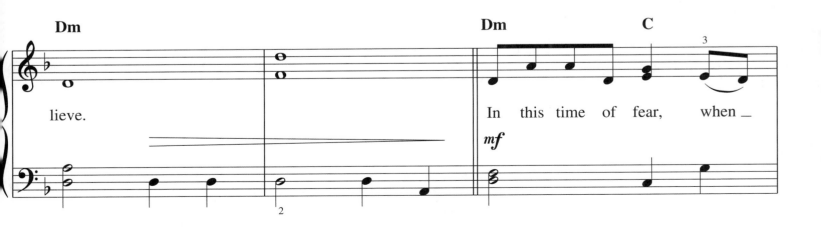

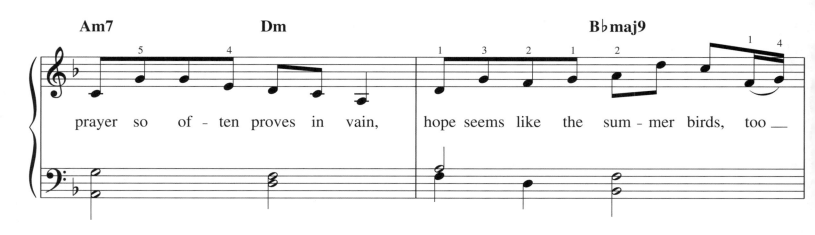

prayer so of - ten proves in vain, hope seems like the sum - mer birds, too __

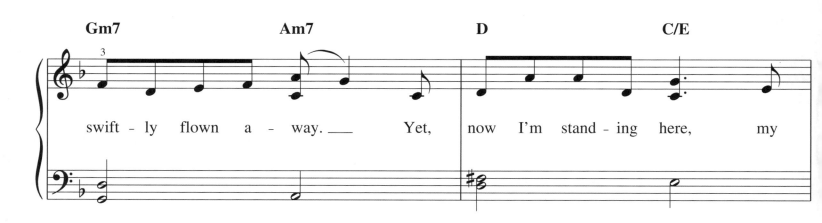

swift - ly flown a - way. __ Yet, now I'm stand - ing here, my

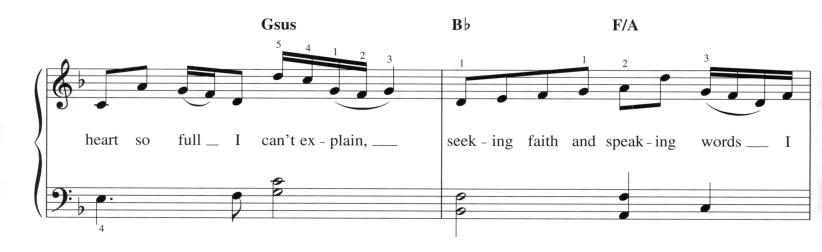

heart so full __ I can't ex - plain, __ seek - ing faith and speak - ing words __ I

nev - er thought I'd say: __ There can be mir - a - cles

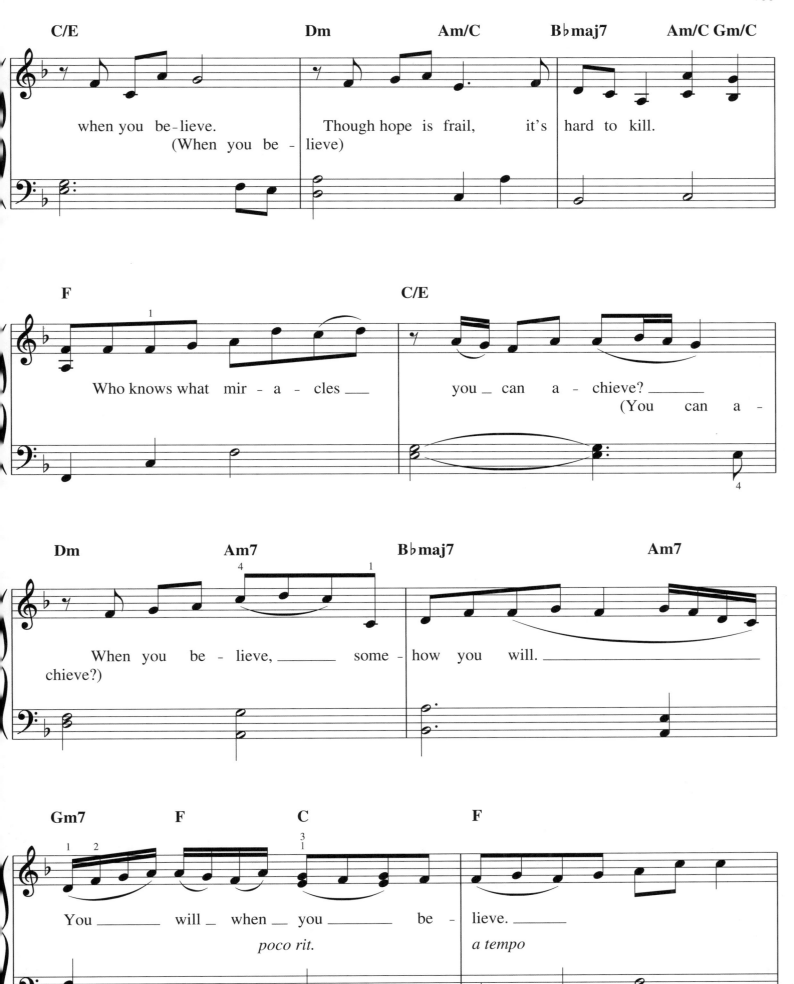

They don't

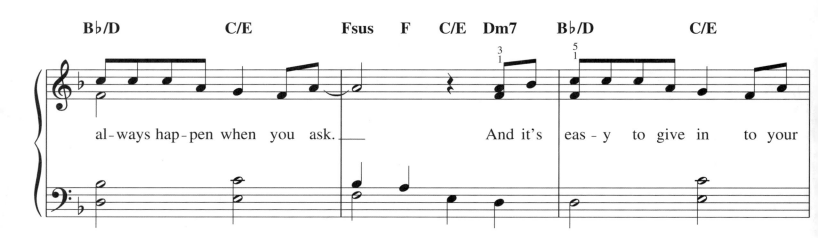

al-ways hap-pen when you ask.___ And it's eas-y to give in to your

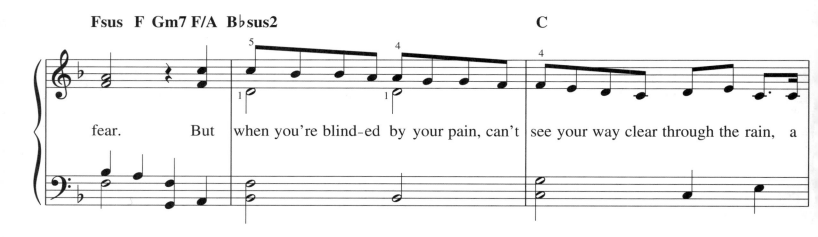

fear. But when you're blind-ed by your pain, can't see your way clear through the rain, a

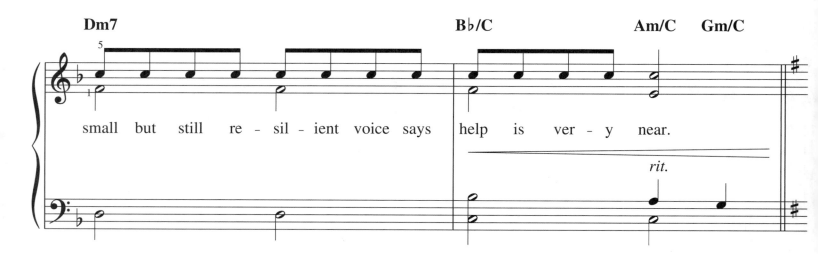

small but still re-sil-ient voice says help is ver-y near.

rit.

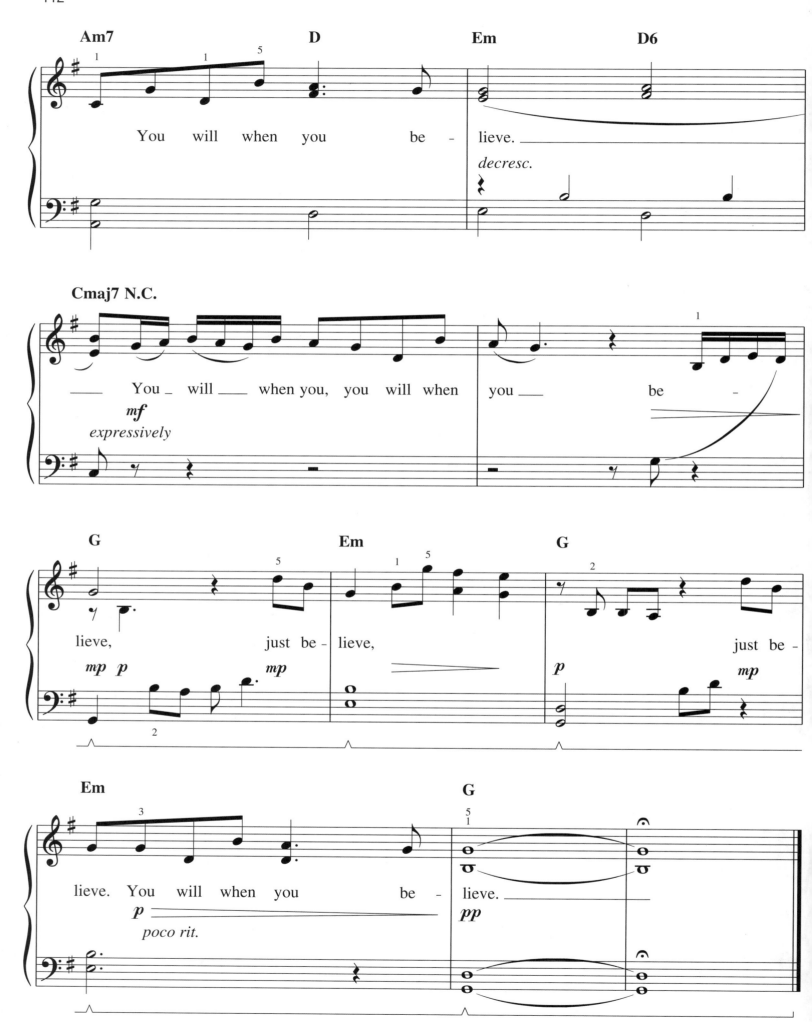

YOU RAISE ME UP

Words and Music by BRENDAN GRAHAM
and ROLF LOVLAND

Moderately slow

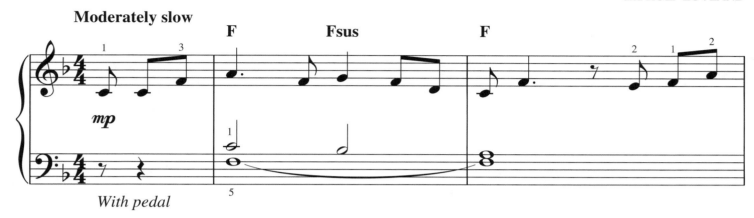

With pedal

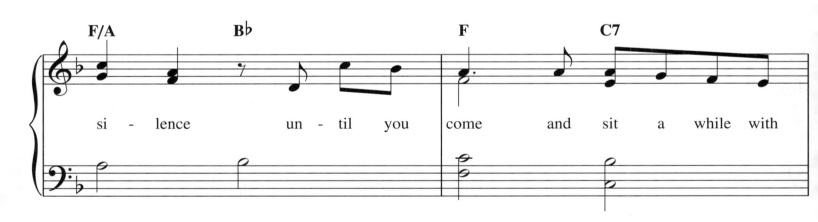

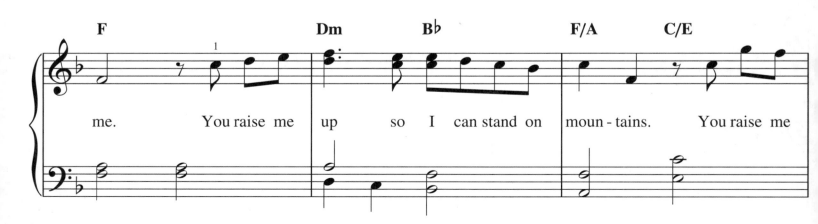

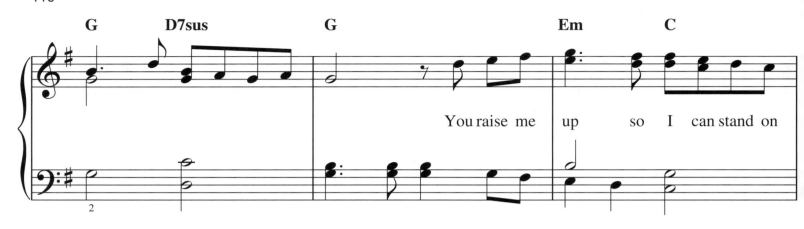

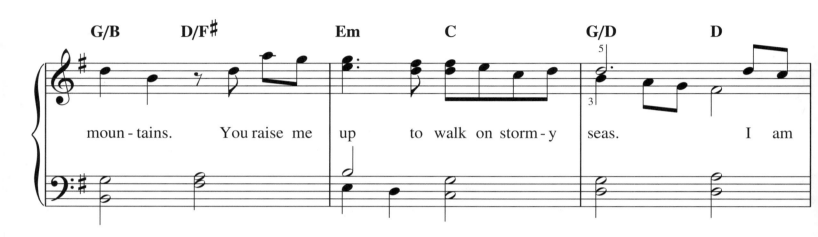

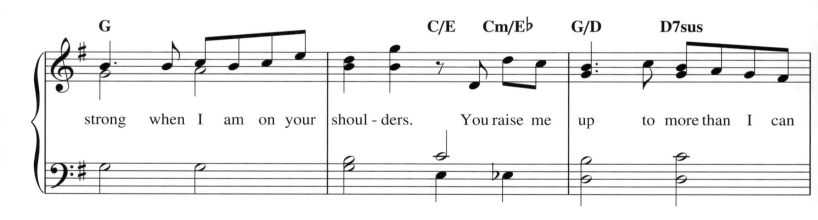

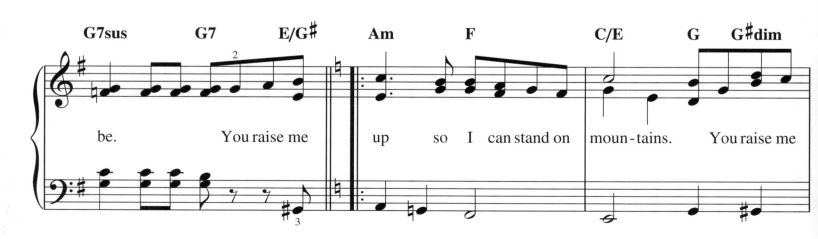

YOU LIGHT UP MY LIFE

Words and Music by
JOSEPH BROOKS

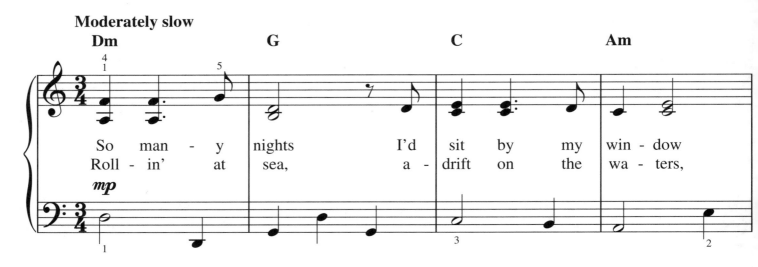

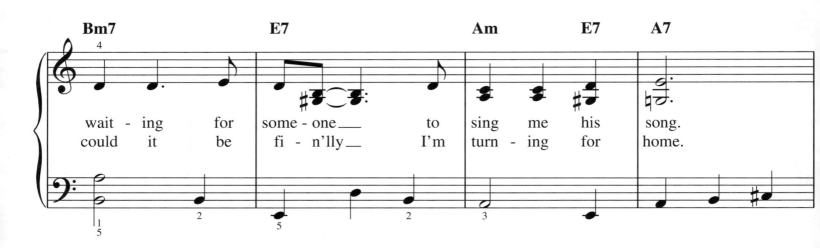

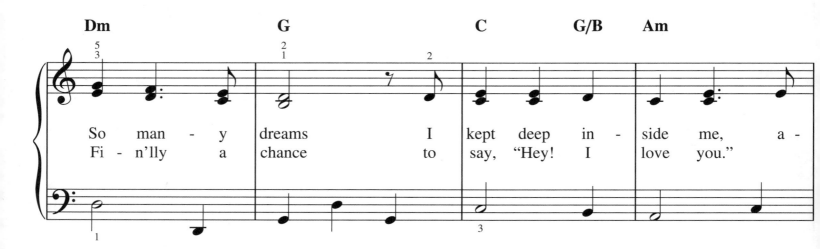

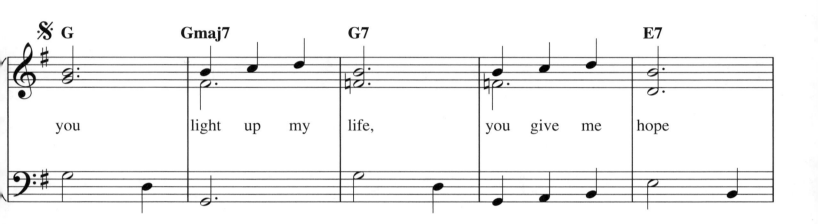

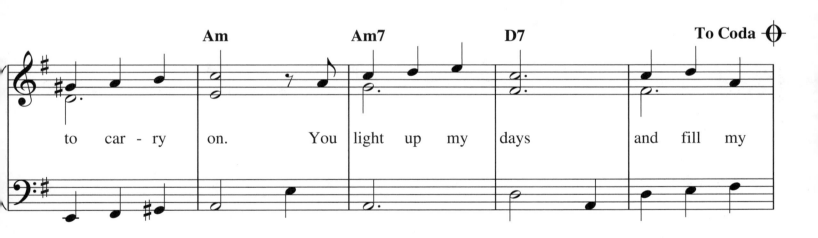

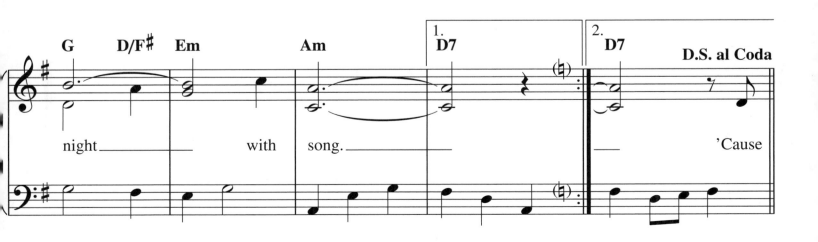

CODA

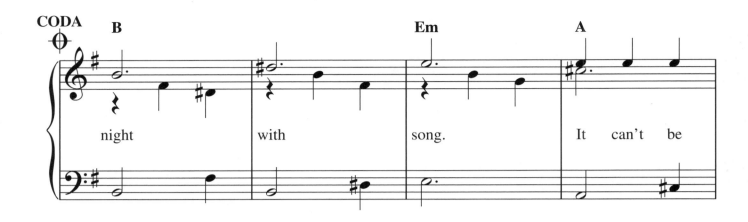

night   with   song.   It can't be

wrong_____ when   it   feels   so   right,_____   'cause

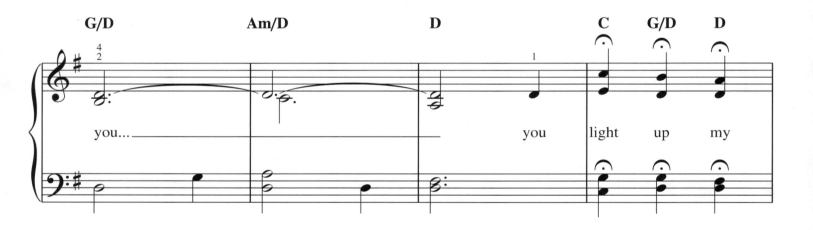

you..._____ you   light   up   my

life._____ *rit.*